PSALMS FOR T[
AND
SONGS FROM THE PSALMS
COMBINED WORDS EDITION

Edited by Michael Perry
with David Iliff and David Peacock

in association with CPAS

Hodder & Stoughton
LONDON SYDNEY AUCKLAND TORONTO

Also from Jubilate Hymns, published by Hodder and Stoughton:

Hymns for Today's Church
Carols for Today
Church Family Worship
Psalms for Today – Full Music Edition
Songs from the Psalms – Full Music Edition

Copyright Information
Every effort to trace copyright-holders and to obtain permission has been made; the publishers
would welcome details of any errors or omissions. Corrections will be incorporated into future
reprints. This title is available in the USA from Hope Publishing Company, Carol Stream, Illinois
60188, USA.

British Library Cataloguing in Publication Data

Perry, Michael, *1942–*
Psalms for today and songs from the psalms. – Combined words ed.
  I. Title   II. Iliff, David   III. Peacock, David
  223.2052

ISBN 0 340 52242 9

CONTENTS

PREFACE

'Sing to the God of our salvation!'

The Psalms have come down to us as a treasure-store of spiritual encouragement. In them the grace of God is revealed and through them we are able to express our wonder and adoration. They inspire both art and music, they give us words for celebration, and they match our moods of joy and sadness.

Individual psalms are very different: some speak of kings and victories, others offer sensitive words to those who are at the end of their resources. Some are designed for large congregations celebrating, with the aid of drama, the great acts of God in the history of salvation; others are vehicles of individual piety. The psalms are God's provision for worship. We must not neglect such gracious gifts. *Psalms for Today* and *Songs from the Psalms* challenge us once again to find a central place in our worship for this resource from the word of God.

This combined words edition is matched by separate music books in order to give expression to the texts in the wide range of musical idiom in use today. The Jubilate spoken ('Liturgical') psalms are included in the text and at the back of both music books; these provide rhythmic and participatory alternatives for the minister and congregation to use. It is hoped that those who approach this present edition through *Songs from the Psalms* might soon discover the contrasting style and added riches of *Psalms for Today*, and vice versa.

The music books *Psalms for Today* and *Songs from the Psalms* also include a host of directory and musical performance aids, together with full musical acknowledgements and addresses of major copyright-holders.

We acknowledge the work of song-writers who have found inspiration in setting the Scriptures to music. We owe special thanks to Michael Baughen, Chairman of Jubilate Hymns and Bishop of Chester, who began this series with *Psalm Praise* – a pioneering book which opened the door to the psalms for many, and encouraged a new generation of word-smiths and musicians to attempt settings for today's church.

We offer this volume along with the music editions of *Psalms for Today*, and *Songs from the Psalms* to English-speaking Christians – for their delight, and for the praise of our glorious God.

MICHAEL PERRY

1A

From Psalm 1
© Michael Perry/Jubilate Hymns

1 If we love the word of God
    and heed it day and night;
  if we make God's truth our law,
    God's counsel our delight:

2 If we shun the sinners' way
    and spurn their false advice;
  if we turn from Godless lies
    and evils that entice:

3 If we do these things we'll find
    rich blessings as we go;
  then we'll flourish like a tree
    where living waters flow.

2 Blessed are they,
    for as a tree by streams of water
    spreads its leaves
    in bountiful displays,
    bears and yields its ripened fruit
        in season –
    so shall they in every calling
    prosper all their days.

3 Blessed are they
    though sinners like the chaff be scattered,
    blessed are they
    though winds of judgement blow;
    from the Lord,
        upon his righteous servants,
    loving care and tender mercies
    evermore shall flow.

1B

From Psalm 1
© Brian Foley

1 The Law of God is life to choose,
  the Will of God is joy to see,
  the Word of God is truth to speak,
  the Love of God brings love to be!

2 The Law of God is no mere list
  of things to do and not to do,
  but God's perfection – this alone
  the yes and no of all we do!

WOMEN
3 The Will of God must be our will,
  to wish, to want, to do, to be;
  and with the mind of God, to think,
  and through the eyes of God, to see!

MEN
4 The Word of God, the voice of God,
  was through his Servant-Prophets heard,
  in time, foretelling One-to-Come –
  his Servant-Son, his living Word!

ALL
5 The Love of God is God himself –
  most precious gift that he can give! –
  to be in us the cause of love,
  to fill with love the life we live!

6 Then make the Law of God our law,
  the Will of God our chosen ways,
  the Word of God our firmest faith,
  and God himself our endless praise!

1C

From Psalm 1
© Paul Wigmore/Jubilate Hymns

1 Blessed are they
  who listen not to evil counsel,
  turn aside
  from every thought of sin:
  day and night, the law of God their maker
  is their joy and meditation,
  well of life within.

1D

From Psalm 1
© Michael Perry/Jubilate Hymns

1 When we walk with God, we are blessed:
    not the wicked and their schemes,
    nor the evil and their dreams –
  when we walk with God,
    (yes) we are blessed.

2 When we trust in God, we are blessed:
    when his law is our delight,
    and we heed it day and night –
  when we trust in God,
    (yes) we are blessed.

3 When we feed on God, we are blessed:
    like a growing tree in place
    by the flowing streams of grace –
  when we feed on God,
    (yes) we are blessed.

4 When we walk with God, we are blessed:
    for the Lord is at our side
    as our strength, our hope, our guide –
  when we walk with God,
    (yes) we are blessed.

1E

From Psalm 1
© Michael Baughen/Jubilate Hymns

1 Bless-ed is the man,
    the man who does not walk
    in the counsel of the ungodly –
    bless-ed is that man;
  he who rejects the way,
    rejects the way of sin
  and who turns away from scoffing –
    bless-ed is that man:
    but his delight
    by day and night
  is the law of God almighty.

2 He is like a tree –
  a tree that flourishes
being planted by the water –
  bless-ed is that man.
He will bring forth fruit –
  his leaf will wither not,
for in all he does he prospers –
  bless-ed is that man:
    for his delight
    by day and night
is the law of God almighty.

3 The ungodly are not so
    for they are like the chaff
which the wind blows clean away –
    the ungodly are not so;
the ungodly will not stand
    upon the judgement day
nor belong to God's own people –
    the ungodly will not stand:
      but God knows the way
      of righteous men
and ungodly ways will perish.

  Bless-ed is the man,
    the man who does not walk
  in the counsel of the ungodly –
    bless-ed is that man!

1F From Psalm 1
       © Michael Perry/Jubilate Hymns

1 God is with the righteous –
  they shall not be moved;
God is with the righteous –
  they shall not be moved:
just like a tree growing by the river-side
they shall not be moved.
  WOMEN They shall not –
    MEN they shall not be moved;
  WOMEN they shall not –
    MEN they shall not be moved:
    ALL just like a tree growing
         by the river-side
         they shall not be moved!

2 God condemns the wicked –
  they shall be removed;
God condemns the wicked –
  they shall be removed:
just like the chaff
            blowing in the wind all day
they shall be removed.
  WOMEN They shall be –
    MEN they shall be removed;
  WOMEN they shall be –
    MEN they shall be removed:
    ALL just like the chaff
         blowing in the wind all day
         they shall be removed!

3 Happy when we hear him –
  we shall not be moved;
happy when we hear him –
  we shall not be moved:
just like a tree growing by the river-side
we shall not be moved.
  WOMEN We shall not –
    MEN we shall not be moved;
  WOMEN we shall not –
    MEN we shall not be moved:
    ALL just like a tree
              growing by the river-side
         we shall not be moved!

4 Happy when we love him . . .

5 Happy when we serve him . . .

6 When we read the Bible . . .

7 If we follow Jesus . . .

3A From Psalm 3
       © Christopher Idle/Jubilate Hymns

1 How many are against me, Lord:
  how many fierce attacks rise up!
  They say 'God will not come to help'
  and people taunt, 'There is no hope.'

2 But you are round me, Lord, my shield;
  but you, my glory, lift my head!
  You hear me from your holy hill
  and answer when I cry aloud.

3 I go to rest, and sleep in peace –
  I wake again; God keeps me safe:
  ten thousand shall not make me fear,
  for all their threats to take my life.

4 Arise, O Lord, to rescue me:
  arise and save me, O my God!
  You silence all my enemies
  till scorn and spite are all destroyed.

5 Your blessings, Father, grant to us;
  your help, O Saviour, still be ours:
  O Holy Spirit, fill our lives –
  to God be glory, love, and praise!

3B From Psalm 3
       © International Bible Society

SOLO
1 O Lord, how many are my foes,
  how many rise against me;
  how many say of me that
  'God will not deliver him'!

ALL
2 But you are a shield around me, Lord,
  my glorious One, who lifts up my head.
  To the Lord I cry aloud,
  and from his holy hill he answers me.

3 I lie down in sleep –
   but I wake again, sustained by the Lord.
   I will not fear ten thousand men
   drawn up against me on every side.

4 Arise, O Lord, deliver me,
   for I have seen you deal with
        your enemies.
   From the Lord deliverance comes:
   may your blessing be on all your people.

4A From Psalm 4
   © Christopher Idle/Jubilate Hymns

1 O God, defender of the poor,
   have mercy when I pray:
   you listened to my prayer before –
   Lord, hear my prayer today!

2 How long will people choose vain things,
   love empty words and wrong?
   They scorn to serve the King of kings –
   O living God, how long?

3 The saints, O Lord, you set apart
   by grace to be your own:
   let sinners tremble, search their hearts,
   and bow before your throne.

WOMEN
4 While many pray that you will bless
   and bring them all they need,
   unless they long for holiness
   their prayers are vain indeed.

MEN
5 Your light, O Lord, let us receive,
   your face within us shine:
   for richer is the joy you give
   than all their corn and wine.

ALL
6 And even when I turn to sleep
   your blessings still increase,
   for you alone, O Lord, will keep
   your child in perfect peace.

4B From Psalm 4
   © Margaret Wilson

1 O righteous Lord who set me right,
   who broke all bonds and led me out
   from black despair to boundless hope:
   be gracious now and hear my prayer.

2 They turn away from you, my God;
   they look for truth in clever lies,
   no honour give to your great name:
   Lord, hear me when I call to you.

3 Many demand a clear-cut sign:
   'O that God's hand might bring us good!'
   Yet to my heart you bring more joy
   than they derive from all their gain.

4 Lord, teach them how you sought us out,
   and set your sign upon our hearts;
   teach them to rest in silent trust,
   shine on them with your glorious light.

5 O Lord, my Lord, who gave me joy
   surpassing all that wealth can bring:
   in peace I lie, in peace I sleep,
   safe in your care, safe in your care.

5 From Psalm 5, Brian Foley
   © 1971 Faber Music Ltd

1 Lord, as I wake I turn to you,
   yourself the first thought of my day;
   my king, my God, whose help is sure,
   yourself the help for which I pray.

2 There is no blessing, Lord, from you
   for those who make their will their way,
   no praise for those who will not praise,
   no peace for those who will not pray.

3 Your loving gifts of grace to me,
   those favours I could never earn,
   call for my thanks in praise and prayer,
   call me to love you in return.

4 Lord, make my life a life of love,
   keep me from sin in all I do;
   Lord, make your law my only law,
   your will my will, for love of you.

6 From Psalm 6
   © Michael Perry/Jubilate Hymns

1 O gracious Lord, be near me!
   My soul cries out, 'How long?
   When will you turn to hear me
   and save your child from wrong?'

2 'How shall the voice you gave me
   sing praises from the dead?
   Return, O Lord, and save me;
   in love lift up my head.'

3 I knew the fear of dying,
   and sorrow filled my eyes;
   but God who hears my crying,
   in judgement will arise!

7A From Psalm 7
   © Michael Perry/Jubilate Hymns

      I will give thanks to the Lord most high;
      I will sing praise to his righteous name.

1 I have no strength but yours,
   O God, my hiding-place;
   you snatch me from the lion's claws
   and save me by your grace.
      I will give thanks . . .

2 To love that will not cease
  I owe my life, my all;
  and justly if I break God's peace
  then punishment will fall.
    I will give thanks to the Lord most high;
    I will sing praise to his righteous name.

3 My God, my sovereign still,
  my shield, my joy, my crown:
  you honour those who do your will,
  you tread the evil down.
    I will give thanks . . .

7B From Psalm 7
© Michael Perry/Jubilate Hymns

1 I have no strength but yours,
  O God, my hiding-place;
  you snatch me from the lion's claws
  and save me by your grace.
    I will give thanks to the Lord most high;
    I will sing praise to his righteous name.
    I will give thanks to the Lord,
    I will sing praise to his name.

2 To love that will not cease
  I owe my life, my all;
  and justly if I break God's peace
  then punishment will fall.
    I will give thanks . . .

3 My God, my sovereign still,
  my shield, my joy, my crown:
  you honour those who do your will,
  you tread the evil down.
    I will give thanks . . .

8A From Psalm 8, Fred Kaan
© Stainer & Bell Ltd

1 Lord, how majestic is your name!
  The earth and sky adore you,
  the mouths of babies sing your praise
  and children dance before you.

2 When I look up and see the stars
  and think of space unending,
  I marvel that you come and care,
  us with your love befriending.

3 You lift us to the very height
  of your creative likeness,
  just as you raised your Son from death
  to Easter's wideawakeness.

8B From Psalm 8, Brian Foley
© 1971 Faber Music Ltd

1 With wonder, Lord, we see your works,
  we see the beauty you have made;
  this earth, the skies, all things that are
  in beauty made.

2 With wonder, Lord, we see your works,
  and child-like in our joy we sing
  to praise you, bless you, maker, Lord
  of everything.

3 The stars that fill the skies above,
  the sun and moon which give our light,
  are your designing for our use
  and our delight.

4 We praise your works, yet we ourselves
  are works of wonder made by you;
  not far from you in all we are
  and all we do.

5 All you have made is ours to rule,
  the birds and beasts at will to tame,
  all things to order for the glory
  of your name.

8C Psalm 8, © David Frost
Pointing © Wm Collins

1 O ' Lord our ' Governor:
  **how glorious is your ' name
  in ' all the ' earth!**
2 Your majesty above the heavens is ' yet
  re'counted:
  **by the ' mouths
    of ' babes and ' sucklings.**

Second part
3 You have founded a strong defence
  a'gainst your ' adversaries:
  **to quell the ' ene·my '
  and · the a'venger.**

4 When I consider your heavens the '
  work of · your ' fingers:
  **the moon and the stars
  which ' you have ' set in ' order,**
5 what is man   that you should be '
  mindful ' of him:
  **or the son of ' man
  that ' you should ' care for him?**

6 Yet you have made him little ' less · than
  a ' god:
  **and have ' crowned him ·
  with ' glory · and ' honour.**
7 You have made him the ' master · of
  your ' handiwork:
  **and have put all things in sub'jection ·
    be'neath his ' feet,**

8 all ' sheep and ' oxen:
  and all the ' creatures ' of the ' field,
9 the birds of the air and the ' fish · of the '
  sea:
  **and everything that moves
  in the pathways '
    of the ' great ' waters.**

Second part
10 O ¹ Lord our ¹ Governor:
   **how glorious is your ¹ name
      in ¹ all the ¹ earth!**

   **Glory to the Father and ¹ to the ¹ Son:
   and ¹ to the ¹ Holy ¹ Spirit;
   as it was in the be¹ginning · is ¹ now:
   and shall be for ¹ ever. ¹ A¹men.**

8D

From Psalm 8, Michael Smith
© 1981 Meadowgreen Music Co.

O Lord, our Lord,
how majestic is your name in all the earth;
O Lord, our Lord,
how majestic is your name in all the earth;
O Lord, we praise your name;
O Lord, we magnify your name.
Prince of peace, mighty God,
O Lord God almighty!

8E

From Psalm 8
© Michael Perry/Jubilate Hymns

1 Sovereign Lord, in all the earth
   how majestic is your name!
   Infant voices from their birth
      fervent praise proclaim,
      fervent praise proclaim.

2 When I lift my eyes I see
   all the stars you set in place:
   who am I that I should be
      favoured by such grace,
      favoured by such grace?

3 Yet you prove to us your love
   and exalt us very high,
   making us as lords above
      earth and sea and sky,
      earth and sea and sky.

4 Sing aloud our saviour's worth –
   mercy, truth, and love proclaim:
   Sovereign Lord, in all the earth
      holy is your name,
      holy is your name!

8L

Psalm 8.1–9
© Editor/Jubilate Hymns

O Lord, our Lord:
**how great is your name
   in all the world!**
A **Your glory fills the skies.**
B **Your praise is sung by children.**
C **You silence your enemies.**

I look at the sky your hands have made,
the moon and the stars you put in place:
ALL **Who are we that you care for us?**

You made us less than gods:
ALL **to crown us with glory and honour.**

You put us in charge of creation:
A **the beasts of the field.**
B **the birds of the air.**
C **the fish of the sea.**

O Lord, our Lord:
ALL **how great is your name
   in all the world!**

   **Glory to the Father, and to the Son,
   and to the Holy Spirit:
   as it was in the beginning, is now,
   and shall be for ever. Amen.**

The congregation may divide at A, B *and* C.

9

From Psalm 9
© Michael Perry/Jubilate Hymns

   I praise you, Lord, with all my heart,
   rejoicing in your wonders!

1 Your justice is perfect
   (your justice is perfect),
   your judgements are true
   (your judgements are true);
   the wicked have fallen
   (the wicked have fallen),
   their names are forgotten
   (their names are forgotten).
      I praise you, Lord . . .

2 You govern the peoples
   (you govern the peoples),
   you help the oppressed
   (you help the oppressed);
   and no-one who seeks you
   (and no-one who seeks you)
   is ever forsaken
   (is ever forsaken).
      I praise you, Lord . . .

10

From Psalm 10
© Timothy Dudley-Smith

1 In my hour of grief or need
   when a friend is friend indeed,
   now, when Satan walks abroad,
   be not far from me, O Lord.

2 When the powers of evil ride
   through the world in open pride,
   flaunted sins and boasted shame
   bring contempt upon your name –

3 When the godless man is strong;
   when his mouth is filled with wrong,
   bitterness, deceit and fraud,
   be not far from me, O Lord.

4 When the poor becomes his prey,
   when the weak are led astray,
   right is wrong and truth is lies –
   then, O Lord our God, arise!

5 Powers of darkness bring to grief,
   break the hold of unbelief,
   sound anew the quickening word –
   rise and come among us, Lord!

6 Then shall vice and falsehood fail,
   truth and righteousness prevail,
   all his ransomed people sing
   God, their everlasting King!

11 From Psalm 11
© Basil Bridge

1 I find my refuge in the Lord,
   no fears shall make me fly away:
   the mountains hide the hunted bird;
   his truth stands firm – with him I stay.

2 The Lord is in his holy place,
   enthroned on high, yet near at hand;
   both saint and sinner come to face
   his judgement, in his presence stand.

3 He knows what I through shame conceal,
   yet offers me this cup of grace:
   his Spirit's fire will cleanse and heal,
   the upright shall behold his face.

12A From Psalm 12
© Michael Perry/Jubilate Hymns

   God will arise
   because the weak are crying,
   God will arise
   because the needy call,
   God will arise
   who knows and loves them all.

1 Flawless are God's mighty words –
   silver forged in fire,
   shaming every evil tongue,
   every dark desire.
     God will arise . . .

2 When the wicked strut about,
   when they take the sword,
   hear your people in their pain,
   come to us, O Lord!
     God will arise . . .

12B From Psalm 12
© Keith Landis

1 The promises of God are pure,
   as tempered steel made keen and sure,
   by hammer-blows forged to endure,
     a sword for my defending.

2 The promises of God remind
   my soul of silver well-refined,
   a matchless cup by Love designed,
     divine elixir blending.

3 The promises of God are right,
   as finest gold, most precious, bright,
   superbly wrought for my delight,
     a crown of life unending.

13A From Psalm 13
© Christopher Idle/Jubilate Hymns

1 How long will you forget me, Lord,
   and hide your face away?
   How long shall evils tear my heart
   and troubles fill my day?

2 Look on my need, O Lord my God
   who grants my every breath;
   give light that I may see your light,
   not sleep the sleep of death.

3 Look on their threats and hear my cry,
   and answer when I call:
   or they will claim the victory
   who long to see me fall.

4 But since I trust your constant love
   my heart is glad and free
   to sing the praises of the Lord
   for all your grace to me.

13B From Psalm 13
© Michael Saward/Jubilate Hymns

1 Forgotten for eternity –
   is that to be my destiny?
   Your face no more to smile on me,
   oppressed by every enemy,
   my soul enduring agony?
     Oh answer me, my God;
     oh answer me, my God!

2 Restore to me serenity
   and, in your gracious charity,
   lest I should die, give light to me;
   frustrate my gloating adversary,
   uplift my soul in ecstasy,
     and I'll rejoice, my God;
     and I'll rejoice, my God!

13C From Psalm 13
© Barbara Woollett/Jubilate Hymns

1 How long, O Lord,
   will you forget
   an answer to my prayer?
   No tokens of your love I see,
   your face is turned away from me;
     I wrestle with despair.

2 How long, O Lord,
   will you forsake
   and leave me in this way?
   When will you come to my relief?
   My heart is overwhelmed with grief,
     by evil night and day.

3 How long, O Lord –
   but you forgive,
   with mercy from above.
   I find that all your ways are just,
   I learn to praise you and to trust
     in your unfailing love.

14
From Psalm 14
© Stephen Wilcockson

1 The fool whose heart declares in pride,
   'There is no God to fear,'
   forgets the Lord's all-seeing eye
   who finds no goodness here:

2 For all have sinned and turned from God,
   not one has kept God's way;
   corrupt alike, not one does good –
   we all have gone astray.

3 Do they not know, can they not tell,
   who plan to crush the poor,
   that God is with the righteous still,
   their refuge ever sure?

4 Now come, O Lord, your people bless,
   and purify from wrong,
   that we may make your righteousness
   our everlasting song!

15A
From Psalm 15
© Paul Wigmore/Jubilate Hymns

1 Lord, who may dwell within your house
     and on your holy hill?
   All those who walk a blameless way,
   who love the right, who win the day
   with truthful words and, come what may,
     will speak no word of ill:

2 All those who love their neighbour well,
     who hate the way of sin,
   who honour all that fear the Lord,
   whose promise is a binding cord,
   who help, and seek no rich reward –
     these, Lord, you welcome in.

15B
From Psalm 15
© David Preston/Jubilate Hymns

1 Lord, who may venture where you dwell,
   or worship on your holy hill?
   The pure in heart, whose spotless lives
   by word and deed obey your will.

2 They never do their neighbour wrong,
   and utter no malicious word;
   the sinner's folly they despise,
   but honour those who fear the Lord.

3 They keep their oath at any cost,
   and gladly lend, but not for gain;
   they hate all bribery: come what may,
   secure for ever they remain.

16A
From Psalm 16
© Owen Dowling

1 I set the Lord before my eyes,
   and look in longing to him;
   Christ calls me daily to arise
   from fear and anxious striving.
   At my right hand he always moves,
   the path through darkened places shows,
   his hold is firm, consoling.

2 The One who takes the fear from death
   turns darkness into dawning;
   my spirit and my mind give birth
   to praises fresh each morning.
   All nightly fears will now depart,
   for hope secure within the heart
   is found with Christ's appearing.

16B
From Psalm 16, Mike Kerry
© 1982 Thankyou Music

   In your presence is fullness of joy,
   fullness of joy, fullness of joy;
   at your right hand
     are pleasures for ever,
   pleasures for evermore.

   I keep the Lord before me,
   I shall not be moved;
   my heart is glad and my soul rejoices,
   I shall dwell in safety.
     And in your presence . . .

16C
From Psalm 16, Martin Nystrom
© 1984 Integrity's Hosanna! Music

   I will come and bow down at your feet,
     Lord Jesus;
   in your presence is fullness of joy.
   There is nothing, there is no-one
     to compare with you;
   I take pleasure in worshipping you, Lord.

16D
From Psalm 16
© Norman Warren/Jubilate Hymns

You will show me the path of life;
you will show me the path of life.

1 In your presence,
in your presence
are pleasures evermore,
pleasures evermore.
You will show me . . .

2 At your right hand,
at your right hand are joys for evermore,
joys for evermore.
You will show me . . .

17
From Psalm 17
© David Mowbray/Jubilate Hymns

1 Lord of all my footsteps,
watching from above,
keep me in the safety
of your perfect love.

2 Others moved by malice
spread untruths around:
shall their schemes not falter
and their plans rebound?

3 For their hope is riches,
time will yet destroy;
you are all my treasure
and my lasting joy.

18A
From Psalm 18
© Christopher Idle/Jubilate Hymns

1 I love you, O Lord, you alone,
my refuge on whom I depend;
my maker, my saviour, my own,
my hope and my trust without end.
The Lord is my strength and my song,
defender and guide of my ways;
my master to whom I belong,
my God who shall have all my praise.

2 The dangers of death gathered round,
the waves of destruction came near;
but in my despairing I found
the Lord who released me from fear.
I called for his help in my pain,
to God my salvation I cried;
he brought me his comfort again,
I live by the strength he supplied.

3 The earth and the elements shake
with thunder and lightning and hail;
the cliffs and the mountain-tops break
and mortals are feeble and pale.
His justice is full and complete,
his mercy to us has no end;
the clouds are a path for his feet,
he comes on the wings of the wind.

4 My hope is the promise he gives,
my life is secure in his hand;
I shall not be lost, for he lives!
He comes to my aid – I shall stand!
Lord God, you are powerful to save,
your Spirit will spur me to pray;
your Son has defeated the grave:
I trust and I praise you today!

18B
From Psalm 18
© Keith Landis

1 I love you, Lord, my strength and rock,
my health and vigour, heartbeat, breath,
my fortress and deliverer
from death of life and life of death!

2 My God, my refuge and my shield,
my stronghold and salvation's door;
Lord Christ, most worthy to be praised,
all these you are, yet more – much more!

18C
From Psalm 18
© Michael Perry/Jubilate Hymns

I love you, O Lord,
my Rock and my Redeemer,
for you make me strong;
I trust in you always.
You are my shield,
the hope of my salvation;
I cry out to you,
and offer you my praise.

1 The seas of death –
their torrents overwhelm me;
in my perplexity I call upon the Lord;
and from his heaven
he hears my voice and rescues me,
he reaches down and saves me
by his word.
I love you, O Lord . . .

2 The mountains shake –
they tremble at his anger,
like burning coals
their fire consumes the skies;
he tears the clouds,
the lightning strikes his enemies,
he guides me in the way
and makes me wise.
I love you, O Lord . . .

3 My Saviour lives –
    his mercy has delivered me,
    he raised me up to this exalted place;
    I worship him who makes me share
        his victories
    and evermore will follow me with grace.
    I love you, O Lord . . .

19A

From Psalm 19, Fred Pratt Green
© Stainer & Bell Ltd

1 We look into your heavens and see
    your glory in creation –
    there's not a sun or galaxy
    but speaks our adoration.

2 We look into our wayward hearts:
    how wisely you direct us!
    Your law is where our justice starts,
    its clear commands protect us.

3 From mercy what have I to hide?
    You hold me back from sinning.
    O let me not be ruled by pride,
    where sin has its beginning.

4 That you approve my spoken word,
    my thoughts and my behaviour,
    will be your servant's great reward,
    my Sun, my Shield, my Saviour!

19B

From Psalm 19
© Christopher Idle/Jubilate Hymns

1 Glory and praise to God!
    All the skies sing praise –
    songs from the sun and moon,
    from the nights and days:

    No human voice is there,
    no mortal speech is heard;
    still through the depths of space
    speeds the sounding word.

    Up comes the morning sun
    for his mighty race,
    and the Lord shines on us
    with his truth and grace.

2 Glory and praise to God
    for his perfect law,
    making the simple wise
    and the waverer sure.

    Sweeter than honeycomb,
    richer than purest gold;
    praise for redemption's plan
    which the words unfold.

    Lord, keep my heart from sin –
    you have set me free:
    be my life and my light;
    Jesus, shine on me.

19C

From Psalm 19, Carl P Daw Jnr
© 1982, 1988 Hope Publishing Company

1 God's glory fills the heavens with hymns,
    the domed sky bears the Maker's mark;
    new praises sound from day to day
    and echo through the knowing dark.
    Without a word their songs roll on –
    into all lands their voices run;
    and with a champion's strength and grace
    from farthest heaven comes forth the sun.

2 God's perfect law revives the soul,
    its precepts make the simple wise,
    its just commands rejoice the heart,
    its truth gives light unto the eyes.
    For ever shall this law endure –
    unblemished, righteous, true, complete;
    no gold was ever found so fine,
    no honey in the comb more sweet.

3 God's servant may I ever be –
    this world my joy, that word my guide:
    O cleanse me, Lord, from secret sin;
    deliver me from selfish pride.
    Accept my thoughts
        and words and deeds;
    let them find favour in your sight –
    for you alone can make me whole,
    O Lord my refuge and my might.

19D

From Psalm 19
© Barbara Woollett/Jubilate Hymns

1 Everywhere the skies declare
    the glory of the Lord!
    Day after day they shout his praise,
    night after night they show his ways;
    everywhere their voice is heard,
        in every corner of the world –
        the glory of the Lord,
        the glory of the Lord!

2 Everywhere the sun declares
    the glory of the Lord!
    And like a bridegroom in his fame,
    a champion running in the game,
    everywhere it shines abroad,
        in every corner of the world –
        the glory of the Lord,
        the glory of the Lord!

3 Everywhere his word declares
    the glory of the Lord!
    His perfect law revives the soul,
    his promises our hearts console;
    everywhere his voice is heard,
        in every corner of the world –
        the glory of the Lord,
        the glory of the Lord!

4 Everywhere his saints declare
the glory of the Lord!
And they don't try to hide their blame,
but come to him in Jesus' name;
everywhere their lives record,
    in every corner of the world –
    the glory of the Lord,
    the glory of the Lord!

19E

From Psalm 19, Bob Fraser
© 1985 Ears and Eyes Music Ltd/
Boosey & Hawkes Music Publishers Ltd

May the words of my mouth,
the meditation of my heart,
be always acceptable to you, O Lord;
may the words of my mouth,
the meditation of my heart,
be always acceptable to you, O Lord;
    O Lord, my rock and my redeemer,
    O Lord, my strength and my shield!

May the words . . .

May the words of my mouth,
the meditation of my heart,
be always acceptable to you.

19F

From Psalm 19, Graham Kendrick
© 1988 Make Way Music/Thankyou Music

May our worship be acceptable
    in your sight, O Lord;
may our worship be acceptable
    in your sight, O Lord;
may the words of my mouth be pure,
    and the meditation of my heart;
may our worship be acceptable
    in your sight, O Lord.

20A

From Psalm 20
© Michael Perry/Jubilate Hymns

1 May the Lord God hear you pray,
    may God's strength be yours today;
    may God bless you from above,
    lifting up your heart in love.

2 May God give you all you need,
    may God make your plans succeed;
    may God guide you all your days,
    filling all our hearts with praise:

3 Now we see the Lord can save,
    now the trembling heart is brave;
    now we know that Love will hear:
    worship now, for God is near!

20B

From Psalm 20, Philip Lawson-Johnston
© 1984 Thankyou Music

May the Lord answer you
    when you are in distress,
may the name of God protect you;
may he send you help from the sanctuary
and grant you support from Zion.

May he give to you
    the desire of your heart
and make all your plans succeed:
we will shout for joy
    when we see you victorious,
and we'll lift up our banners
    in the name of our God!

    Some will trust in earthly power,
    some will trust in man,
    but we will trust
        in the name of our God.
    They are brought down to their knees,
    they are doomed to fall,
    but we rise up and stand firm.

May the Lord . . .

    O Lord, deliver us,
    answer when we call.
    O Lord, deliver us,
    answer when we call.

May he give to you
    the desire of your heart
and make all your plans succeed:
we will shout for joy
    when we see you victorious,
and we'll lift up our banners
    in the name of our God!

May the Lord grant your requests.

20C

From Psalm 20
© Michael Perry/Jubilate Hymns

1   MEN May the Lord God
                hear your prayer,
   WOMEN may the Lord God
                hear your prayer;
    MEN may his name protect you always,
  WOMEN may his name protect you always!
    ALL May he meet you in his house,
            lifting up your heart in worship,
                in worship;
            lifting up your heart in worship.

2   MEN May he grant your true desire,
   WOMEN may he grant your true desire;
   MEN may he make your plans
          successful,
   WOMEN may he make your plans
          successful!
   ALL may he give you all you need,
      causing everyone to thank him,
      to thank him;
      causing everyone to thank him.

3   MEN Now we know the Lord can save,
   WOMEN now we know the Lord can save;
   MEN now we trust this world no longer,
   WOMEN now we trust this world no longer.
   ALL Now we see he answers prayer:
      praise him now for all his mercy,
      his mercy;
      praise him now for all his mercy!

20D

From Psalm 20, John Pantry
© 1987 Ears and Eyes Music Ltd/
Boosey & Hawkes Music Publishers Ltd

1 Some trust in chariots,
      some in their horses;
  but we will trust in the name of the Lord.
  All those who lean on
      their own understanding
  will be brought to their knees
      and shall fall.
    But the saving power
    of God's right hand
    will never fail;
    the saving power
    of God's right hand
    will never fail.

2 Long may he grant
      the desires of your heart,
  and with power make all of your plans
      to succeed.
  We'll shout for joy
      when we hear of your victories,
  lift up our banners and sing!
    But the saving power
    of God's right hand
    will never fail;
    the saving power
    of God's right hand
    will never fail.

3 May the Lord hear you
      whenever you're troubled,
  send to you help and give you new heart;
  if you can trust in him, he will direct you,
  and your feet will not fall from the path.

But the saving power
of God's right hand
will never fail;
the saving power
of God's right hand
will never fail.
But the saving power . . .

21

From Psalm 21
© David Mowbray/Jubilate Hymns

1 With all your heart rejoice, and sing
  to God the Lord of all!
  His mercy, like a mountain spring,
  brings life to great and small.

2 A happy king who trusts in God,
  his shining crown secure!
  His face is bright, his prayers are heard,
  his throne shall long endure.

3 Yet who, except the Lord most high,
  may bear the eternal name,
  or reign in unspoilt majesty
  above our worldly shame?

4 The King of kings, the Christ of God,
  to whom all power is given!
  Rise, then, with spirit undeterred,
  and join the praise of heaven!

22A

From Psalm 22
© Brian Foley

1 Why, God, have you forsaken me –
  more distant now the more I cry?
  Must I, alone unanswered, go
  like one unloved, alone to die?

2 Our fathers when they prayed to you
  in every need, in every prayer,
  were heard by you and saved by you,
  and never doubted that you care!

MEN
3 But now my people turn on me
  with hate, not pity, in their eyes;
  and all who see me, see in me
  no man, a worm that they despise!

WOMEN
4 Let God deliver him, they say;
  his God would save him, was his claim!
  They only wait to see me die;
  they share my clothing in a game!

MEN
5 My hands and feet they bind to wound;
  my bones they number, and each breath,
  until with burning thirst I taste
  the bitter agony of death!

6   My God, I trust you, trust you still –
    be near, be near to hear my prayer!
    I know that all who hope in you
    are safe in death from death's despair.

ALL

7   Then I and all who live for you,
    this day and till the end of days,
    will tell of ever-answered prayer,
    and pray this world's
            most thankful praise!

22B

From Psalm 22, Brent Chambers
© 1977 Scripture in Song/Thankyou Music

In the presence of your people
  I will praise your name,
for alone you are holy,
  enthroned on the praises of Israel.
Let us celebrate your goodness
  and your steadfast love;
may your name be exalted
  here on earth and in heaven above!

Lai, lai . . .

22C

From Psalm 22, John Bell
© The Iona Community/
Wild Goose Publications

ALL

O Lord my God, O Lord my God,
why do you seem so far from me,
O Lord my God?

CHOIR

1   Night and morning I make my prayer:
    peace for this place, and help for there;
      waiting and wondering,
      waiting and wondering –
    does God care; does God care?
      ALL O Lord my God . . .

CHOIR

2   Pain and suffering unbound and blind
    plague the progress of humankind,
      always demanding,
      always demanding –
    does God mind; does God mind?
      ALL O Lord my God . . .

CHOIR

3   Why, oh why do the wicked thrive,
    poor folk perish, the rich survive;
      begging the question,
      begging the question –
    is God alive; is God alive?
      ALL O Lord my God . . .

CHOIR

4   Turn again as you hear my plea,
    tend the torment in all I see;
      loving and healing,
      loving and healing –
    set me free, set me free!
      ALL O Lord my God . . .

23A

From Psalm 23
© Christopher Idle/Jubilate Hymns

1   The Lord my shepherd rules my life
    and gives me all I need;
    he leads me by refreshing streams,
    in pastures green I feed.

2   The Lord revives my failing strength,
    he makes my joy complete;
    and in right paths, for his name's sake,
    he guides my faltering feet.

3   Though in a valley dark as death,
    no evil makes me fear;
    your shepherd's staff protects my way,
    for you are with me there.

4   While all my enemies look on
    you spread a royal feast;
    you fill my cup, anoint my head,
    and treat me as your guest.

5   Your goodness and your gracious love
    pursue me all my days;
    your house, O Lord, shall be my home –
    your name, my endless praise.

6   To Father, Son and Spirit, praise!
    to God, whom we adore,
    be worship, glory, power and love,
    both now and evermore!

23B

From Psalm 23
© Pearl Beasley/Jubilate Hymns

1   O Lord my shepherd,
            lead me in your ways
    to cooling streams
            where I shall drink and live;
    to pastures green
            where I may spend my days
    in perfect peace that only you can give.

2   When deepest darkness
            falls around my head,
    I need not fear with you close by my side;
    and all along the stony road I tread
    you will be there
            to strengthen and to guide.

3 You welcome me to share the holy feast,
  you offer me forgiveness and your love;
  and with your goodness
        all my days are blessed –
  until at last I reach your home above.

23C
Psalm 23, © David Frost
Pointing © Wm Collins

1 The Lord ' is my ' shepherd:
  therefore ' can I ' lack ' nothing.
2 He will make me lie down in ' green '
  pastures:
  and ' lead me · be'side still ' waters.

3 He will re'fresh my ' soul:
  and guide me in right pathways '
  for his ' name's ' sake.
4 Though I walk through the valley of the
  shadow of death I will ' fear no ' evil:
  for you are with me *
  your ' rod · and your ' staff '
      comfort me.

5 You spread a table before me *
  in the face of ' those who ' trouble me:
  you have anointed my head with oil '
  and my ' cup · will be ' full.
6 Surely your goodness and loving-
  kindness will follow me * all the ' days · of
  my ' life:
  and I shall dwell
  in the ' house · of the ' Lord for ' ever.

  Glory to the Father and ' to the ' Son:
  and ' to the ' Holy ' Spirit;
  as it was in the be'ginning · is ' now:
  and shall be for ' ever. ' A'men.

23D
From Psalm 23, H W Baker (1821–1877)
© in this version Jubilate Hymns

1 The king of love my shepherd is,
  whose goodness fails me never;
  I nothing lack if I am his
  and he is mine for ever.

2 Where streams of living water flow,
  a ransomed soul, he leads me;
  and where the fertile pastures grow,
  with food from heaven feeds me.

3 Perverse and foolish I have strayed,
  but in his love he sought me;
  and on his shoulder gently laid,
  and home, rejoicing, brought me.

4 In death's dark vale I fear no ill
  with you, dear Lord, beside me;
  your rod and staff my comfort still,
  your cross before to guide me.

5 You spread a banquet in my sight
  of love beyond all knowing;
  and O the gladness and delight
  from your pure chalice flowing!

6 And so through all the length of days
  your goodness fails me never:
  Good Shepherd, may I sing your praise
  within your house for ever!

23E
From Psalm 23, Bob Fraser
© 1987 Ears and Eyes Music Ltd/
Boosey & Hawkes Music Publishers Ltd

  The Lord is my shepherd –
  he knows the things I need;
  though I go through deepest darkness
  he will guide and he will lead.
  The Lord is my shepherd –
  I will not be afraid;
  his goodness and his mercy
  will never, never fade.

1 You guide me on the right path –
  I know you'll always care;
  and when I need protection,
  your rod and staff are there.
    The Lord is my shepherd . . .

2 And even though surrounded
  by every enemy,
  you've got the banquet ready,
  so everyone can see.
    The Lord is my shepherd . . .

23F
From Psalm 23
© 1985 Christopher Walker

1 Because the Lord is my shepherd
  I have everything I need;
  he lets me rest in the meadow
  and leads me to the quiet streams;
  he restores my soul
  and he leads me
        in the paths that are right.
  Lord, you are my shepherd,
  you are my friend:
  I want to follow you always –
  just to follow my friend.

2 And when the road leads to darkness,
  I shall walk there unafraid;
  even when death is close
  I have courage, for your help is there;
  you are close beside me with comfort,
  you are guiding my way.
    Lord, you are my shepherd . . .

3 In love you make me a banquet
   for my enemies to see;
   you make me welcome,
   pouring down honour
         from your mighty hand;
   and this joy fills me with gladness –
   it is too much to bear.
      Lord, you are my shepherd,
      you are my friend;
      I want to follow you always –
      just to follow my friend.

4 Your goodness always is with me,
   and your mercy I know;
   your loving-kindness
         strengthens me always
   as I go through life;
   I shall dwell in your presence for ever,
   giving praise to your name.
      Lord, you are my shepherd . . .

24A From Psalm 24
© David Mowbray/Jubilate Hymns

1 Lift up your heads, eternal gates:
   the Lord our God draws near;
   the King of glory now awaits,
   his hosts in strength appear.

2 What mortal dare ascend God's hill
   or reach that holy place?
   Not those who plan their neighbours ill
   and bring them to disgrace.

3 Yes, all the earth is God's alone,
   its compass far and wide,
   and in that King upon the throne
   our trust and hope reside.

24B From Psalm 24
© Michael Perry/Jubilate Hymns

      Fling wide the gates,
      unbar the ancient doors;
      salute your king
      in his triumphant cause!

1 Now all the world
         belongs to Christ our Lord:
   let all creation greet the living Word!
      Fling wide . . .

2 Who has the right to worship him today?
   All those who gladly serve him and obey.
      Fling wide . . .

3 He comes to save
         all those who trust his name,
   and will declare them
         free from guilt and shame.
      Fling wide . . .

4 Who is the victor glorious from the fight?
   He is our king, our life, our Lord,
         our right!
      Fling wide . . .

24C Psalm 24, © David Frost
Pointing © Wm Collins

1 The earth is the Lord's and ' all · that is '
   in it:
   the compass of the ' world
   and ' those who ' dwell therein.
2 For he has founded it up'on the ' seas:
   and es'tablished it · up'on the ' waters.

3 Who shall ascend the ' hill · of the ' Lord:
   or who shall ' stand ·
      in his ' holy ' place?
4 He that has clean hands and a ' pure '
   heart:
   who has not set his soul upon idols *
   nor ' sworn his ' oath · to a ' lie.

5 He shall receive ' blessing · from the '
   Lord:
   and recompense
   from the ' God of ' his sal'vation.
6 Of such a kind as this are ' those who '
   seek him:
   those who seek your ' face
   O ' God of ' Jacob.

7 Lift up your heads O you gates * and
   be lifted up you ever'lasting ' doors:
   and the King of ' glory '
      shall come ' in.
8 Who is the ' King of ' glory?
   the Lord strong and mighty *
   the ' Lord ' mighty · in ' battle.

9 Lift up your heads O you gates * and
   be lifted up you ever'lasting ' doors:
   and the King of ' glory '
      shall come ' in.
10 Who is the ' King of ' glory?
   the Lord of hosts '
   he · is the ' King of ' glory.

   Glory to the Father and ' to the ' Son:
   and ' to the ' Holy ' Spirit;
   as it was in the be'ginning · is ' now:
   and shall be for ' ever. ' A'men.

24D

From Psalm 24
© Christopher Idle/Jubilate Hymns

1 This earth belongs to God,
the world, its wealth, and all its people;
he formed the waters wide
and fashioned every sea and shore.
  A Who may go up the hill of the Lord
    and stand in the place of holiness?
  B Only the one whose heart is pure,
    whose hands and lips are clean.

2 Lift high your heads, you gates;
rise up, you everlasting doors,
as here now the King of glory
enters into full command.
  A Who is the King, this King of glory,
    where is the throne he comes to claim?
  B Christ is the King, the Lord of glory,
    fresh from his victory.

3 Lift high your heads, you gates,
and fling wide open the ancient doors,
for here comes the King of glory
taking universal power.
  A Who is the King, this King of glory,
    what is the power by which he reigns?
  B Christ is the King, his cross his glory,
    and by love he rules.

4 All glory be to God
the Father, Son, and Holy Spirit;
from ages past it was,
is now, and evermore shall be.

The singers may divide at A and B.

24E

From Psalm 24, Michelle Stoodley
© 1978/9 Mustard Seed Music

  Lift up your heads, O you gates,
  and be lifted up, O ancient doors,
  that the King of glory may come in.
    Lift up your heads . . .

1 The earth is the Lord's
    and the fullness thereof,
the world and those who dwell therein;
he has founded it upon the seas
and has established it upon the rivers.
    Lift up your heads . . .

2 Who shall ascend the hill of the Lord
and stand in his holy place?
He who has clean hands and a pure heart,
who does not lift up his soul
    to what is false.
    Lift up your heads . . .

3 The blessing of the Lord is theirs,
and peace from the God of their salvation:
such is the people who seek him,
who seek the face of the God of Jacob.
    Lift up your heads . . .

4 Who is the King of glory?
The Lord strong and mighty in battle!
Who is this King of glory?
The Lord of hosts is his name.
    Lift up your heads . . .

24F

From Psalm 24, Graham Kendrick
© 1986 Make Way Music/Thankyou Music

    MEN The earth is the Lord's
 WOMEN and everything in it.
    MEN The earth is the Lord's
 WOMEN the work of his hands.
    MEN The earth is the Lord's
 WOMEN and everything in it:
    ALL and all things
        were made for his glory!

1 The mountains are his,
the seas and the islands,
the cities and towns,
the houses and streets:
let rebels bow down
and worship before him,
for all things were made for his glory!
    MEN The earth is the Lord's . . .

2 The mountains are his . . .

    MEN The earth is the Lord's
 WOMEN and everything in it.
    MEN The earth is the Lord's
 WOMEN the work of his hands.
    MEN The earth is the Lord's
 WOMEN and everything in it:
    ALL and all things were made,
        yes, all things were made,
        and all things were
           made for his glory!

24G

From Psalm 24
© Adrian Cleaton

1 The earth and its fullness
    belong to God alone;
we worship our maker
    who's seated on his throne.
He formed the earth and founded it
    upon the deepest sea:
O worship our Creator God,
the master of all eternity!

2 But who on the earth
    can ascend God's holy hill?
  Or who in his presence
    can stand serene and still?
  The one whose hands and heart
        are clean,
    whose soul is humble too:
  O worship him, our loving God,
  whose justice and faithfulness are true!

3 So lift up your heads,
    O you mighty doors and gates:
  the King who is glorious
    outside the city waits.
  Who is this King of glory then?
    The Lord of victory!
  O worship him, so strong in war,
  triumphant in might and majesty!

4 Then lift up your heads,
    O you ancient doors and gates:
  the great King of glory
    outside the city waits.
  Who is this King of glory then?
    The mighty God is he!
  O worship him, the King of kings,
  the sovereign of all eternity!

24H

From Psalm 24, Graham Kendrick
© 1988 Make Way Music/Thankyou Music

1 ALL Fling wide your doors,
            O you streets;
        open up, you hearts of men,
        that the King of glory may come in;
        fling wide your doors,
            O you streets;
        open up, you hearts of men,
        that the King of glory may come in!

   WOMEN Who is this King of glory?
     MEN The Lord, strong and mighty.
   WOMEN Who is this King,
            this King of glory?
     MEN The Lord – his name is Jesus!

2 ALL Fling wide your doors . . .
   WOMEN Who is . . .

3 ALL Fling wide your doors . . .

   LEADER Fling wide your doors,
      ALL fling wide your doors,
   LEADER O you streets,
      ALL O you streets –
            open up, you hearts of men!
   LEADER Fling wide your doors,
      ALL fling wide your doors,
   LEADER O you streets,
      ALL O you streets –
            open up, you hearts of men!

24I

From Psalm 24, Tom McLain
© 1984 Glory Alleluia Music/Word Music (UK)

  Glory, glory, glory to the King;
  glory, glory, glory to the King!
  Glory . . .

Who is the King of glory?
King Jesus is his name;
he is high and lifted up above the earth,
and his name I will proclaim.
  Glory . . .

24L

Psalm 24.1–10
© Editor/Jubilate Hymns

  The earth is the Lord's, and everything
  in it:
  the world, and all who live here.

  He founded it upon the sea:
  and established it upon the waters.

E Who has the right to go up the Lord's
  hill; who may enter his holy temple?
  **Those who have clean hands
  and a pure heart,
  who do not worship idols
  or swear by what is false.**

  They receive blessing continually from
  the Lord:
  **and righteousness
  from the God of their salvation.**

  Such are the people who seek for God:
  **who enter the presence
      of the God of Jacob.**

D Fling wide the gates, open the ancient
  doors:
  that the king of glory may come in.

E Who is the king of glory?
  **The Lord, strong and mighty,
  the Lord mighty in battle.**

D Fling wide the gates, open the ancient
  doors:
  that the king of glory may come in.

E Who is he, this king of glory?
  **The Lord almighty,
  he is the king of glory.**

  **Glory to the Father, and to the Son,
  and to the Holy Spirit:
  as it was in the beginning, is now,
  and shall be for ever. Amen.**

E – *enquirer*, D – *director, or these lines may
also be said by the minister.*

25A

From Psalm 25
© Timothy Dudley-Smith

1 All my soul to God I raise:
Be my guardian all my days.
Confident in hope I rest,
Daily prove your path is best.
Ever work in me your will,
Faithful to your promise still.

2 Graciously my sins forgive;
Help me by your truth to live.
In your footsteps lead me, Lord,
Joy renewed and hope restored,
Knowing every sin forgiven,
Learning all the ways of heaven.

3 Mercies manifold extend,
Not as judge but faithful friend.
O my Saviour, hear my prayer,
Pluck my feet from every snare;
Quietude be mine at last,
Rest from all my guilty past.

4 Sheltered safe when troubles fret,
Trusting God I triumph yet!
Undismayed in him I stand,
Victor only by his hand.
Worship, homage, love and praise,
All my soul, to God I raise.

WOMEN Show me your ways, O Lord;
MEN show me your ways, O Lord.
WOMEN Teach me your truth, O Lord;
MEN teach me your truth, O Lord –
WOMEN and guide me
in the way that leads to life:
MEN and guide me into life.
WOMEN You are the way, my Lord;
MEN you are the way, my Lord.
WOMEN You are the truth, my Lord;
MEN you are the truth, my Lord –
WOMEN to know you is to have eternal life;
MEN to know you is to have eternal life.

2 Remember, Lord, your mercy and love,
for they have been from of old;
remember not the sins of my youth
or my rebellious ways.
WOMEN Show me your ways . . .

3 O guard my life and rescue me,
let me not be put to shame;
turn to me and be gracious unto me,
for my hope is in your name.
WOMEN Show me your ways . . .

25B

From Psalm 25, Janice A Finn
© 1986 Word Music (UK)

Show me your ways, O Lord;
teach me your paths
and lead me in your truth.

Show me your ways . . .

For you are the God of my salvation,
on you do I wait all the day long;
for you are the God of my salvation,
on you do I wait all the day.

25C

From Psalm 25, Malcolm Scott
© 1987 Ears and Eyes Music Ltd/
Boosey & Hawkes Music Publishers Ltd

1 To you, O Lord, I lift up my soul,
in you I trust, O my God;
more than the watchman
waits for the morn
my soul shall wait for the Lord.

25D

From Psalm 25
Verses: © The Grail/A P Watt Ltd
Chorus: © Paul Inwood/Magnificat Music

ALL Remember, remember
your mercy, Lord;
remember, remember
your mercy, Lord:
hear your people's prayer
as they call to you;
remember, remember
your mercy, Lord.

SOLO
1 Lord, make me know your ways,
Lord, teach me your paths;
make me walk in your truth,
and teach me,
for you are God my saviour.
ALL Remember . . .

SOLO
2 Remember your mercy, Lord,
and the love you have shown from of old;
do not remember the sins of my youth.
In your love remember me,
in your love remember me
because of your goodness, O Lord.
ALL Remember . . .

3 The Lord is good and upright,
   he shows the path to all who stray;
   he guides the humble in the right path,
   he teaches his way to the poor.
   ALL Remember, remember
            your mercy, Lord;
         remember, remember
            your mercy, Lord:
         hear your people's prayer
            as they call to you;
         remember, remember
            your mercy, Lord.

26 From Psalm 26
   © Michael Perry/Jubilee Hymns

1 To lead a blameless life, O Lord,
   to trust you without fear,
   to bring my humble heart to you
   and know your love is near:

2 To walk before you in the truth,
   to shun the evil ways,
   to come into your house to pray
   and shout aloud your praise:

3 Let this be my supreme desire,
   my object and my prayer,
   until I stand before your throne
   to glorify you there!

27A From Psalm 27
   J Montgomery

1 God is my strong salvation –
   what foe have I to fear?
   In darkness and temptation
   my light, my help is near:

2 Though hosts encamp around me,
   firm to the fight I stand!
   What terror can confound me,
   with God at my right hand?

3 Place on the Lord reliance,
   my soul, with courage wait –
   his truth my reassurance
   when faint and desolate:

4 His might my heart shall strengthen,
   his love my joy increase;
   mercy my days shall lengthen,
   the Lord will give me peace.

27B From Psalm 27
   © Michael Perry/Jubilee Hymns

1 Safe in the hands of God who made me,
   what can there be that I should fear?
   God is my light and my salvation,
   strong is his help when foes are near.

2 This I have prayed and will seek after,
   that I may walk with God each day;
   then will he give me his protection,
   no trouble shall my heart dismay.

3 God of my life, my Lord, my master,
   father and mother now to me:
   come, shield me from the threat of evil,
   lift up my soul and set me free!

4 Teach me your way
            and lead me onwards,
   save me from those who do me wrong;
   give me the grace to wait with patience,
   help me to trust, hold firm, be strong.

28 From Psalm 28
   © Michael Perry/Jubilee Hymns

1 O Lord, my rock, to you I cry
   when others will not hear;
   to you I lift my hands on high –
   your arms are always near, O Lord,
   your arms are always near.

2 I grieve for those who keep fine friends
   but harbour Godless schemes;
   who use your works for worthless ends,
   to squander on their dreams, O Lord,
   to squander on their dreams.

3 Yet praise the Lord who comes at length,
   who comes to right the wrong:
   to you our shepherd and our strength
   be praise in joyful song, O Lord,
   be praise in joyful song!

29A From Psalm 29
   © Basil Bridge

1 Let all in heaven and earth unite
      in this, our joyful duty;
   to praise our God, the Lord of might,
      the source of truth and beauty;
   the rumbling thunder's awesome voice,
   the lightning flash, both cry, 'Rejoice!
   Come, give him praise and glory!'

2 God's voice is echoed by the seas,
      in storms, their power unfurling,
   in winds that lash the cedar trees
      and set the desert swirling;
   it stirs the mighty ocean deep,
   the hills like startled cattle leap:
      come, give him praise and glory!

29B

From Psalm 29
© Michael Perry/Jubilate Hymns

1 The God of heaven thunders,
his voice in cadent echoes
resounds above the waters
and all the world sings,
    Glory, glory, glory!

2 The desert writhes in tempest,
wind whips the trees to fury;
the lightning splits the forest,
and flame diffuses
    Glory, glory, glory.

3 The mighty God eternal
is to his throne ascended,
as we who are his people
within these walls cry:
    Glory, glory, glory!

29C

From Psalm 29, Derek Howell
© 1985 Ears and Eyes Music Ltd/
Boosey & Hawkes Music Publishers Ltd

1 Bring your tributes to the Lord of hosts,
praise his glory and power;
worship him in his holiness,
for ever singing glory.
    Glory, alleluia,
    glory to the Lord:
    you who stand in his glory,
    praise the Lord of the storm.

2 In his voice hear the thunder,
for he speaks with all power:
the seas hear its splendour
and they echo with his glory.
    Glory, alleluia, . . .

3 In his voice see the lightning,
for it shakes the dry land:
the trees break before him,
creation shouts in glory.
    Glory, alleluia, . . .

4 His people know his blessing,
he gives strength and peace;
for he reigns eternally –
lift up your voice in glory!
    Glory, alleluia, . . .

30A

From Psalm 30, J E Seddon
© Mrs M Seddon/Jubilate Hymns

1 I worship you, O Lord,
for you have raised me up;
I cried to you for help,
and you restored my life.
You brought me back from death
and saved me from the grave.

WOMEN
2 Sing praises to the Lord,
all those who know his name:
for while his wrath is brief,
his favour knows no end.
Though tears may flow at night,
the morning brings new joy.

MEN
3 I said, 'I am so strong
I never shall be moved!'
But you, Lord, shook my life –
my heart was in distress.
I cried for you to help,
and pleaded for your grace:

ALL
4 My mourning you have turned
to dancing and to joy;
my sadness you dispelled
as gladness filled my soul.
And so I'll sing your praise,
my God, through all my days!

30B

From Psalm 30
© Norman Warren/Jubilate Hymns

1 WOMEN You have changed my sadness
into a joyful dance;
    MEN you have changed my sadness
into a joyful dance.
    ALL You have taken away my sorrow
and surrounded me
with joy;
you have changed my sadness
into a joyful dance.

2 WOMEN So I will not be silent,
I will sing praise to you;
    MEN so I will not be silent,
I will sing praise to you.
    ALL Lord, you are my God,
I will give you thanks
for ever;
so I will not be silent,
I will sing praise to you.

31A

From Psalm 31
© Basil Bridge

1 I come to you for shelter, Lord:
    deliver me from every snare.
In you I find true liberty;
    I rest my spirit in your care.

Your loving-kindness cheers my heart;
    you know the hurts, the deep distress!
My times are in your hand – I trust
    your never-failing faithfulness.

2 Your steadfast love is my defence,
my haven from the strife of tongues.
You see my need, you hear my cry,
you turn my sorrows into songs.

May all your people gladly come,
and seeking, find you and adore:
to Father, Son and Spirit give
all praise and glory evermore.

31B
From Psalm 31
© International Bible Society

SOLO/GROUP
1 How great is the goodness
you have shown
to those who seek your name;
the goodness you give in the sight of all
who seek you as a refuge!
In the rock of your presence
you hide them
safe from all intrigues of men,
and you keep them safe
from cruel tongues.
ALL
Be strong, take courage in your heart,
all of you whose hope is in the Lord;
be strong, take courage in your heart,
all of you whose hope is in the Lord!

SOLO/GROUP
2 Praise to the Lord,
for he has shown his wonderful love
to me!
When I was sure I was far away
you heard my cry for mercy.
Show your love to the Lord,
all of you his saints.
The Lord will preserve the faithful one,
but he will repay the proud in full.
ALL
Be strong, take courage in your heart,
all of you whose hope is in the Lord;
be strong, take courage in your heart,
all of you whose hope is in the Lord!

Be strong . . .

32A
From Psalm 32
© David Mowbray/Jubilate Hymns

1 How glad are those with peace of mind,
their past wrongdoings left behind;
their sins forgiven by the Lord –
they stand, rejoicing in their God!

2 While every wrong lay unconfessed,
their spirits knew no lasting rest;
but shedding tears of honesty
they reached the place of heartfelt joy.

3 With your great wisdom, Lord, we pray,
help us to walk life's path today!
How glad are those with peace of mind,
their past wrongdoings left behind!

32B
From Psalm 32, Bill Batstone
© 1984 Maranatha! Music/Word Music (UK)

Happy is the one whose sin
freely is forgiven,
whose innocence has been declared
by the Lord of heaven!
Happy is the one . . .

1 I cried till I could cry no more
when my guilt in me remained;
I fell beneath the burning sun
till forgiveness brought the rain.
Happy is the one . . .

2 When I let my heart be known
and my confession made,
then I saw your mercy flow
to wash my guilt away.
Happy is the one . . .

3 People, let your voice be heard
in prayer before your God:
he alone can rescue you
from trouble like a flood.
Happy is the one . . .

33A
From Psalm 33
© Paul Wigmore/Jubilate Hymns

1 Bring songs of joy to God the Lord
who saves and keeps you by his word;
bring all your skill to harp and lyre,
delight the Lord with purest sound;
let music high to heaven rebound,
your praising hearts a joyful choir.

2 The Lord's own word is right and true,
unfaithful deeds he will not do;
his justice, righteousness and love
flow freely from his gracious hand,
enriching life till all the land
reveals a holy treasure-trove.

3 By merest breath he brought to birth
the starlit skies about the earth;
to him, the oceans vast and wild
are in their raging little more
than water gathered in a store
or given to a thirsty child.

4 Come, fear the Lord! Hope in his love,
revere his word, his mercy prove;
then you will know his power to save,
to overrule the evil plan.
His watching eyes, since earth began,
care for the lives whose breath he gave.

5 With songs of joy to God the Lord
    who saves and keeps us by his word
  we bring our voices, harp and lyre
    whose music shall to heaven rebound.
  We trust in God: in him is found
    true love that sets our hearts on fire.

33B From Psalm 33, Sarah Lacy
© 1985 Ears and Eyes Music Ltd/
Boosey & Hawkes Music Publishers Ltd

All you that are righteous, shout for joy
what the Lord has done!
Praise him, all you that obey him;
give thanks to him (give thanks),
and sing to him a new song.

1 The Lord's words are true;
    for he is just and righteous.
  When he spoke, the world was created.
  Worship him, you peoples;
  honour him, you nations,
  for the Lord is in control!
    All you that are righteous . . .

2 The Lord looks down from heaven,
  he watches over his people,
  over those who trust in his love.
  We put our hope in the Lord,
        for he is our protector;
  in his name we shall be glad.
    All you that are righteous . . .

33L Psalm 33.1–22
© Editor/Jubilate Hymns

Sing joyfully to the Lord, you righteous:
it is right
        that his people should praise him.

Praise the Lord with the harp:
A **make music to him on the strings.**

Sing to the Lord a new song:
B **play skilfully, and shout for joy.**

For the word of the Lord is right and
true:
ALL **and all his work is faithfulness.**

The Lord loves righteousness and
justice:
A **his endless love fills the earth.**

By the word of the Lord the skies were
formed:
B **his breath created moon and stars.**

Let all the earth fear the Lord:
ALL **the people of the world revere him.**

For he spoke, and it came to be:
A **he commanded, and all was made.**

The Lord holds back the nations:
B **he thwarts their evil intent.**

God's purposes are sure:
ALL **his plans endure for ever.**

Happy is the nation whose God is the
Lord:
A **happy the people he makes his own.**

The eyes of the Lord are on those that
fear him:
B **who trust in his unfailing love.**

We wait in hope for the Lord:
A **he is our help and shield.**

In him our hearts rejoice:
B **we trust his holy name.**

May your constant love be with us, Lord:
ALL **as we put our hope in you. Amen.**

*The congregation – and ministers – may
divide at A and B.*

34A From Psalm 34
© Timothy Dudley-Smith

1 Tell his praise in song and story,
    bless the Lord with heart and voice:
  in my God is all my glory,
    come before him and rejoice.
  Join to praise his name together,
    he who hears his people's cry;
  tell his praise, come wind or weather,
    shining faces lifted high.

2 To the Lord whose love has found them
    cry the poor in their distress;
  swift his angels camped around them
    prove him sure to save and bless.
  God it is who hears our crying
    though the spark of faith be dim:
  taste and see! Beyond denying
    blessed are those who trust in him.

3 Taste and see! In faith draw near him,
    trust the Lord with all your powers;
  seek and serve him, love and fear him,
    life and all its joys are ours –
  true delight in holy living,
    peace and plenty, length of days:
  come, my children, with thanksgiving
    bless the Lord in songs of praise.

4 In our need he walks beside us,
   ears alert to every cry;
watchful eyes to guard and guide us,
   love that whispers, 'It is I.'
Good shall triumph, wrong be righted,
   God has pledged his promised word;
so with ransomed saints united
   join to praise our living Lord.

34B From Psalm 34
© Paul Wigmore/Jubilate Hymns

1 I'll praise the Lord for ever and ever,
my soul shall boast
   of his wonderful name:
   Glorify the Lord with me;
   exalt his name, for great is he!
I'll praise the Lord for ever and ever.

2 I sought the Lord,
    he answered my calling,
delivered me from my innermost fears:
   Glorify the Lord . . .

3 O taste and see
    how gracious the Lord is –
secure are they who take refuge in him:
   Glorify the Lord . . .

4 The Lord redeems
    the faithful who serve him,
and those who trust him
    he never condemns:
   Glorify the Lord . . .

34C From Psalm 34, Phil Rogers
© 1984 Thankyou Music

O taste and see that the Lord is good:
how blessed
    is the man who hides himself in him!
I sought the Lord and he answered me,
and set me free from all my fears.
I will give thanks to him, for he is good;
his steadfast love to me will never end.

I will give thanks . . .

34D From Psalm 34, Graham Kendrick
© 1983 Make Way Music/Thankyou Music

1 Praise to the Lord!
Sing alleluias to the king of all the earth.
Praise to his name!
Let every creature join in the joyful song.

MEN I will praise him,
WOMEN I will praise him;
MEN I will exalt him,
WOMEN I will exalt him –
MEN for his love,
WOMEN for his love,
ALL for his love endures for ever!

2 Praise to the Lord!
The wind and the waves,
the thunder and rain,
display his power:
raise now the shout;
come, lift up your voice
and join with all nature's song.
   MEN I will praise him . . .
   WOMEN I will praise him . . .

3 Praise to the Lord!
O taste and see
his goodness and mercy
never fail.
Praise to his name,
who gives to his children
gifts from his generous hand.
   MEN I will praise him . . .
   WOMEN I will praise him . . .

34E From Psalm 34, Jacques Berthier
© 1982, 1983 & 1984 Taizé/Wm Collins

CONTINUOUS RESPONSE
  Holy, holy, holy Lord.
  holy, holy, holy Lord!
OR:
  Sanctus, sanctus, Dominus,
  sanctus, sanctus, Dominus!

ALTERNATIVE RESPONSE
  Hosanna in the highest,
  hosanna in the highest!
OR:
  Hosanna in excelsis,
  hosanna in excelsis!

SOLO
1 Holy, holy, holy Lord,
   God of power and might:
   heaven and earth
   are full of your glory.
   Hosanna in the highest!

SOLO
2 I will bless the Lord at all times,
   his praise shall always be on my lips:
   glorify the Lord with me,
   together let us praise his name!

36

From Psalm 36
© Christopher Idle/Jubilate Hymns

1 No fear of God before the eyes,
   no penitence within:
   such is the one no longer wise,
   whose words are treachery and lies,
   who never grieves for sin.

2 Your love, O Lord, shall never sleep,
   nor shall your mercy cease;
   your truth is like the mighty deep,
   and like the rocky mountain steep
   your steadfast righteousness.

3 Beneath the shadow of your wings
   our refuge is most sure;
   refreshed by your reviving springs
   and all the joy your mercy brings
   our future is secure.

4 Continue, Lord, your love to me,
   for you are all my trust;
   grant us the light we need, to see
   how good you are, and still shall be
   to those you count as just.

36L

Psalm 36.5–9
© Editor/Jubilate Hymns

   Your love, O Lord, reaches the heavens:
A **your faithfulness extends to the skies.**

   Your righteousness is towering like the
   mountains:
B **your justice is like the great deep.**

   How precious is your love, O God:
A **we find shelter beneath your wings!**

   We feast on the food you provide:
B **we drink
      from the river of your goodness:**

   For with you is the fountain of life:
ALL **in your light we see light. Amen.**

*The congregation – and ministers – may
divide at A and B.*

37A

From Psalm 37
© Michael Perry/Jubilate Hymns

1 Commit your way to God the Lord –
   your cause will shine as bright as fire;
   delight to do God's holy word
   and you shall find what you desire.

2 Be still before the Lord and wait,
   and do not fret when wrong succeeds;
   refrain from anger, turn from hate,
   for God will punish evil deeds.

3 Salvation comes from God alone –
   the faithful know their help is sure;
   to heaven all our needs are known,
   and in God's strength we are secure.

4 Commit your way to God the Lord,
   to peace and truth and grace aspire:
   then mercy shall be your reward,
   God's promises your heart's desire.

37B

From Psalm 37, Edith McNeill
© 1974, 1975 Celebration/Thankyou Music

   The steadfast love of the Lord
      never ceases,
   his mercies never come to an end;
   they are new every morning,
      new every morning:
   great is your faithfulness, O Lord,
   great is your faithfulness!

1 The Lord is my portion, says my soul,
   therefore I will hope in him.
   The steadfast love . . .

2 The Lord is good
      to those who wait for him,
   to the soul that seeks him;
   it is good that we should wait quietly
   for the salvation of the Lord.
   The steadfast love . . .

3 The Lord will not cast off for ever,
   but will have compassion;
   for he does not willingly afflict
   or grieve the sons of men.
   The steadfast love . . .

4 So let us examine all our ways,
   and return to the Lord;
   let us lift up our hearts and hands
   to God in heaven.
   The steadfast love . . .

37C

From Psalm 37, Phil Potter
© Ears and Eyes Music Ltd/
Boosey & Hawkes Music Publishers Ltd

   Delight yourself in the Lord,
   and he'll give you
      the desires of your heart;
   delight yourself in the Lord
   and he'll give you all you need.

   Delight yourself . . .

1 Praise him, thank him, give him love;
   praise him, thank him, give him love.
   Delight yourself . . .

2   Seek him, serve him, give him love;
    seek him, serve him, give him love.
      Delight yourself in the Lord,
      and he'll give you
          the desires of your heart;
      delight yourself in the Lord
      and he'll give you all you need.

      Delight yourself . . .

3   Trust him, follow him, give him love;
    trust him, follow him, give him love.
      Delight yourself . . .

38   From Psalm 38
         © Mollie Knight/Jubilate Hymns

1   Lord, will you turn from your anger
          and hear me?
    Guilt and remorse
          are the burdens I bear;
    When I acknowledge my sin and my folly,
    show your compassion,
          your love and your care.

2   Lord, though my friends and companions
          desert me;
    you will not leave me –
          I know you are near.
    Hear my deep sighing,
          and see my great sorrow –
    you know each secret,
          each longing, each fear.

3   Lord, will you answer
          with words of forgiveness?
    Then shall my joy and my peace
          be restored:
    faithful redeemer and God of all comfort,
    you are my saviour,
          my king and my Lord!

39   From Psalm 39
         © David Mowbray/Jubilate Hymns

1   Silent, I have waited,
      counting out my days;
    questions overwhelm me,
      set my heart ablaze.
    Measured by God's greatness
      human lives are small;
    wealth departs, and beauty
      like a flower will fall.

2   Suffering, leaden-weighted,
      drags my spirit low:
    God in heaven, have mercy,
      let your healing flow!
    All my hope I fasten
      on your strengthening word –
    lift your hand in blessing,
      let my prayer be heard!

40A   From Psalm 40
          © Paul Wigmore/Jubilate Hymns

1   To the Lord I looked in patience
    from the darkest pit of clay,
    for he daily proves his mercy,
    hears my call from far away.
      And I tell the great assembly
      of his goodness night and day.

2   For the Lord I waited, trusting;
    then he turned his loving eye,
    gently lifted me to safety
    on the rock secure and high.
      And a hymn of praise he gave me –
      I shall sing it till I die:

3   O how blessed, my God and Saviour,
    we who trust your mighty hand!
    O how many are the wonders
    which for us your love has planned!
      So shall all who seek and find you
      sing your praise through all the land.

40B   From Psalm 40
          © Michael Baughen/Jubilate Hymns

1   I waited patiently for the Lord,
    he turned and listened to me;
    he drew me out of the echoing pit
    and out of the miry clay.
    He set my feet upon a rock,
    my footsteps he made secure;
    within my mouth he put a new song –
      a song of praise to God,
      a song of praise to God.

2   In many seeing it, fear will come –
    they then will trust in the Lord;
    and he is happy who hopes in the Lord,
    who will not be led astray.
    Your wondrous deeds and thoughts to us
    are multiplied, O my God;
    they number
          more than we can proclaim –
      Lord, none compares with you;
      Lord, none compares with you.

3   It is not offerings you require,
    but open ears to your word;
    and so instead of a sacrifice
    I come to you with my life.
    I love to do your will, O God,
    within my heart is your law;
    deliverance is the news I have told –
      my lips have not been sealed,
      my lips have not been sealed.

4   I have not hidden within my heart
    your steadfast love and your help;
    the congregation have heard me declare
    salvation and faithfulness.
    And so when evils circle me
    have mercy on me, O Lord;
    may all who love you thankfully say,
        The Lord is great indeed,
        the Lord is great indeed!

40C
From Psalm 40, John Bell
© 1987 The Iona Community/
Wild Goose Publications

I waited, I waited on the Lord;
I waited, I waited on the Lord.
He bent down low and remembered me
when he heard my prayer.

40L(i)
Psalm 40.1–3
© Editor/Jubilate Hymns

I waited patiently for the Lord:
he turned and heard my cry.

He pulled me out of the slimy pit:
out of the mud and mire.

He set my feet upon a rock:
and made my step secure.

He put a new song in my mouth:
a hymn of praise to God.

Many will see it and fear;
and put their trust in the Lord. Amen.

40L(ii)
Psalm 40.4–16
© Editor/Jubilate Hymns

Happy are those who trust in God:
who do not worship idols.

Sacrifice and offering you do not desire:
A **but you want my ears to be open.**

So I said, 'Lord I come:
B **obedient to your word.'**

I delight to do your will, O God:
A **and keep your teaching in my heart.**

I'll tell the world your saving news:
B **you know my lips will not be sealed.**

I have not hid your righteousness:
A **but speak of all your salvation, Lord.**

I do not hide your faithful love:
B **but share your mercy with them all.**

May all who come to you be glad; may all
who know your saving power for ever
say:
ALL **How great is the Lord! Amen.**

*The congregation – and ministers – may
divide at* A *and* B.

42A
From Psalm 42
© Keith Landis

1   Like the deer, athirst and questing,
    seeks my soul for God, unresting,
    wide awake or in my dreams,
    longing for life-giving streams.

2   Why on earth should I be fearful,
    foolishly downcast and tearful?
    In my Saviour I have found
    God who keeps me safe and sound.

3   Hope in him, for you will surely
    taste that river flowing purely,
    bright as crystal from his throne,
    God for ever seen and known!

42B
From Psalm 42, © David Frost
Pointing © Jubilate Hymns

CHOIR, then ALL
    O put your trust in God the living God:
    I'll praise him yet,
    my saviour and my God.

1   As a deer longs for the ' running ' brooks:
    so longs my soul for ' you O ' God.
    My soul is thirsty for God *
    thirsty for the ' living ' God:
    when shall I come and ' see his ' face?
    CHOIR, then ALL
        O put your trust . . .

2   My tears have been my food '
    day and ' night:
    while they ask me all day long
    'Where now ' is your ' God?'
    Why are you so full of ' heaviness ·
        my ' soul:
    and why so un'quiet with'in me?
    CHOIR, then ALL
        O put your trust . . .

3   Surely the Lord will grant
        his loving mercy ' in the ' day-time:
    and in the night his song will be with me
    a prayer to the ' God · of my ' life.
    Why are you so full of ' heaviness ·
        my ' soul:
    and why so un'quiet with'in me?
    CHOIR, then ALL
        O put your trust . . .

42c
From Psalm 42, John Bell
© 1989 The Iona Community/
Wild Goose Publications

1 Just as a lost and thirsty deer
   longs for the cool and running stream,
   I thirst for you, the living God,
   anxious to know that you are near.

2 Both day and night I cry aloud;
   tears have become my only food
   while all around cruel voices ask,
   'Where is your God, where is your God?'

3 Broken and hurt I call to mind
   how in the past I served the Lord,
   worshipped and walked
           with happy crowds,
   singing and shouting praise to God.

4 Why am I now so lost and low;
   why am I troubled and confused?
   Given no answer, still I hope
   and trust my Saviour and my God.

42d
From Psalm 42, Martin Nystrom
© 1983 Restoration Music Ltd

1 As the deer pants for the water,
   so my soul longs after you;
   you alone are my heart's desire
   and I long to worship you.
       You alone are my strength, my shield,
       to you alone may my spirit yield;
       you alone are my heart's desire,
       and I long to worship you!

2 I want you more than gold or silver,
   only you can satisfy;
   you alone are the real joy-giver
   and the apple of my eye.
       You alone . . .

3 You're my friend
           and you are my brother,
   even though you are a king;
   I love you more than any other,
   so much more than anything!
       You alone . . .

43a
From Psalm 43
© Keith Landis

1 O Light and Truth of God,
   the world is dark around me;
   deep pitfalls, battlefields,
   and mortal foes surround me:
       you are my Way
       as bright as day –
   all other ways confound me!

2 O high and holy hill,
   O land of peace and resting –
   God's lovely dwelling place,
   the goal of all my questing:
       in you I'll find
       a home assigned,
   a mansion for my guesting!

3 Be not cast down my soul,
   go to his altar singing,
   with instrument and voice
   your gift of music bringing;
       eternal joy
       my lips' employ
   with alleluias ringing!

43b
From Psalm 43
© Michael Perry/Jubilate Hymns

1 When my bitter foes surround,
   when their wicked deeds confound,
   when deceit and lies abound,
       I will hope in God.

2 When deep sorrows overpower,
   when life's pain and doubt devour,
   when I face my darkest hour,
       I will trust in God.

3 Then shall fervent prayers avail,
   then shall light and truth prevail,
   then God's mercy will not fail:
       I will praise my God.

43c
From Psalms 43 and 44
© Rae Ranford/New Wine Music

1 O Father, send your light;
   O Father, send your truth,
   and let them lead me back to you in Zion.
   O Father, send your light;
   O Father, send your truth,
   and let them lead me back to you in Zion.
       I will come to your Temple
       where you live,
       then I'll come to your altar, O God;
       there I'll play my harp
       and sing praise to you –
       you're the source of my happiness.
       Lai, lai, lai . . .

2 You are my God and King
   who gives me everything,
   and in whose name
           I can defeat my enemies.
   I will not trust the bow,
   I will not trust the sword,
   for you have saved me
           from all those who hated me.

My heart yearns for your presence,
mighty God;
my soul thirsts for your righteousness.
I will sing your praise,
I will bless your name –
you're the source of my happiness.
Lai, lai, lai . . .

44

From Psalm 44
© Michael Perry/Jubilate Hymns

1 We have heard, O Lord our God,
the story of your grace:
and how you gave to us this land,
defending us with your right hand
and showing us your face.

2 You are great, O Lord our God,
we trusted in your name;
we did not triumph by the sword,
but through the victory of your word
you put our foes to shame.

3 Yet today, O Lord our God,
the weak – who once were strong –
cry out to you, 'O come, arise,
reveal your light to darkened eyes,
and turn our sighs to song!'

45

From Psalm 45
© David Mowbray/Jubilate Hymns

1 Let those with voices sing,
as if inspired to write
the praises of our king,
our heart and soul's delight:
    Before his throne the nations fall
    and throng to crown him Lord of all.

2 With sceptre in his hand
our king will reign in peace;
no evil can withstand
his sword of righteousness.
    Before his throne . . .

3 Anointed thus to serve,
and set apart on high,
our king yet stoops to love,
to hear his people's cry.
    Before his throne . . .

4 So let his palace ring
with royal praise today;
let sons and daughters bring
their gifts without delay!
    Before his throne . . .

46A

From Psalm 46
© Richard Bewes/Jubilate Hymns

1 God is our strength and refuge,
our present help in trouble;
and we therefore will not fear,
though the earth should change!
Though mountains shake and tremble,
though swirling floods are raging,
God the Lord of hosts
    is with us evermore!

2 There is a flowing river
within God's holy city;
God is in the midst of her –
she shall not be moved!
God's help is swiftly given,
thrones vanish at his presence –
God the Lord of hosts
    is with us evermore!

3 Come, see the works of our maker,
learn of his deeds all-powerful:
wars will cease across the world
when he shatters the spear!
Be still and know your creator,
uplift him in the nations –
God the Lord of hosts
    is with us evermore!

46B

Psalm 46, © David Frost
Pointing © Wm Collins

1 God is our ǀ refuge · and ǀ strength:
   a very ǀ present ǀ help in ǀ trouble.
2 Therefore we will not fear though the ǀ
   earth be ǀ moved:
   **and though the mountains
   are ǀ shaken ·
   in the ǀ midst · of the ǀ sea;**

Second part
3 though the waters ǀ rage and ǀ foam:
   **and though the mountains quake
   at the ǀ rising ǀ of the ǀ sea.**

4 There is a river whose streams make
   glad the ǀ city · of ǀ God:
   **the holy dwelling-place ǀ
   of the ǀ Most ǀ High.**
5 God is in the midst of her *
   therefore she shall ǀ not be ǀ moved:
   **God will ǀ help her ·
   and at ǀ break of ǀ day.**
6 The nations make uproar and the ǀ
   kingdoms · are ǀ shaken:
   **but God has lifted his ǀ voice ·
   and the ǀ earth shall ǀ tremble.**
7 **The Lord of ǀ hosts is ǀ with us:
   the God of ǀ Jacob ǀ is our ǀ stronghold.**

8 Come then and see what the ⁞ Lord has ⁞
done:
what destruction
he has ⁞ brought up⁞on the ⁞ earth.
9 He makes wars to cease in ⁞ all the ⁞
world:
he breaks the bow
and shatters the spear *
and burns the ⁞ chari·ots ⁞ in the ⁞ fire.
10 'Be still and know that ⁞ I am ⁞ God:
I will be exalted among the nations *
I will be ex⁞alted · up⁞on the ⁞ earth.'
11 **The Lord of ⁞ hosts is ⁞ with us:**
the God of ⁞ Jacob ⁞ is our ⁞ stronghold.

Glory to the Father and ⁞ to the ⁞ Son:
and ⁞ to the ⁞ Holy ⁞ Spirit;
as it was in the be⁞ginning · is ⁞ now:
and shall be for ⁞ ever. ⁞ A⁞men.

46C
From Psalm 46
Author unknown

1 Be still and know that I am God,
be still and know that I am God,
be still and know that I am God.

2 The Lord almighty is our God . . .

3 The God of Jacob is our rock . . .

46D
From Psalm 46, Dave Fellingham
© 1985 Thankyou Music

Emmanuel, God is with us,
Emmanuel, God is with us.
The Lord of hosts, he is with us,
the God of Jacob is our stronghold;
the Lord most high
is our refuge and strength.
God is with us, God is with us,
dwelling in the midst of his people;
God is with us, God is with us,
making glad the city of God
as the river of life flows from the throne.
bringing life and strength to all.
We shall not be moved;
God is with us,
Emmanuel, God with us,
God is now with us.

46E
From Psalms 46 and 1, Garth Hewitt
© 1974 Word Music (UK)

1 'Be still and know that I am God;
I stand among you and I am God.
Though the mountains crumble
and disappear
I will be with you – you need not fear.'

2 There's a river of joy flows on and on,
flows through the city –
it's the Father's song;
there's a tree of life by the riverside,
the leaves are for healing
where the tears have been cried.

3 'Be still and know . . .

46L
Psalm 46.1–11
© Editor/Jubilate Hymns

God is our refuge and our strength:
an ever-present help in trouble.

Therefore we will not fear:
A **though the earth should shake,**
B **though the mountains fall into the sea,**
A **though the waters surge and foam,**
B **though the mountains shake and roar.**

The Lord almighty is with us:
ALL **the God of Jacob is our fortress.**

There is a river whose streams make
glad the city of God: the holy place
where the Most High dwells.
A **God is within her, she will not fall:**
B **God will help her at break of day.**

Nations are in uproar, kingdoms fall:
A **God lifts his voice –**
B **the earth melts away.**

The Lord Almighty is with us:
ALL **the God of Jacob is our fortress.**

Come and see what God has done:
his devastation on the earth!

He stops the wars throughout the world:
A **he breaks the bow**
and shatters the spear –
B **he sets the shield on fire.**

V Be still, and know that I am God: I will be
exalted over the nations, I will be exalted
over the earth.

The Lord Almighty is with us:
ALL **the God of Jacob is our fortress.**
Amen.

*The congregation may divide at A and B; V
can be a distant voice, or said by the
minister.*

47A
From Psalm 47
© David Mowbray/Jubilate Hymns

1 Take heart and praise our God;
rejoice and clap your hands –
his power our foe subdued,
his mercy ever stands:

let trumpets sound and people sing,
the Lord through all the earth is king!

2 Take heart, but sing with fear,
exalt his worthy name;
with mind alert and clear
now celebrate his fame:
    let trumpets sound . . .

3 Take heart for future days,
for tasks as yet unknown –
the God whose name we praise
is seated on the throne:
    let trumpets sound . . .

4 Take heart and trust in God
the Father and the Son –
God is our strength and shield,
his Spirit guides us on:
    let trumpets sound . . .

47B From Psalm 47 © David Frost

CHOIR
God is the king of all the earth –
O praise him in a well-wrought psalm.
ALL
God is the king of all the earth –
O praise him in a well-wrought psalm.

1 O clap your hands, all you peoples,
and cry aloud to God with shouts of joy:
for the Lord Most High is to be feared –
he is a great king over all the earth.
    God is the king . . .

2 He cast down peoples under us,
and the nations beneath our feet;
he chose us a land for our possession
that was the pride of Jacob
        whom he loved.
    God is the king . . .

3 God has gone up
        with the sound of rejoicing,
and the Lord to the blast of the horn:
O sing praises, sing praises to God;
O sing praises, sing praises to our King.
    God is the king . . .
    God is the king . . .

47C From Psalm 47, Jimmy Owens © 1972 Lexicon Music Inc/MPI Ltd

Clap your hands, all you people;
shout to our God with a voice of triumph!
Clap your hands, all you people;
shout to our God with a voice of praise!

Hosanna, hosanna:
shout to our God with a voice of triumph!
Praise him, praise him:
shout to our God with a voice of praise!

47D From Psalm 47 © Melva Lea

Sing praises to our God, sing praises;
sing praises to our God, sing praises;
sing praises to our God, sing praises;
Alleluia!

Sing praises . . .

For God is the king over all the earth:
sing praises now to him
        with understanding;
O clap your hands and shout,
        all you people,
for he is to be greatly praised.
    Sing praises . . .

47E From Psalm 47, Herbert Chappell © 1974 Chappell Music Ltd

SOLO
Clap your hands, clap your hands;
shout to God with the voice of triumph.

ALL
Clap your hands, clap your hands;
shout to God with the voice of triumph.

SOLO
For the Lord most high is powerful –
he's the king of all the earth.

ALL
For the Lord most high is powerful –
he's the king of all the earth.

SOLO
He'll subdue the people under us,
and the nations under our feet.

ALL
He'll subdue the people under us,
and the nations under our feet.

*   SOLO
God is gone up with a shout,
and the Lord with sound of trumpets.

ALL
God is gone up with a shout,
and the Lord with sound of trumpets.

SOLO
Clap your hands, clap your hands,
shout to God with the voice of triumph.

Clap your hands, clap your hands,
shout to God with the voice of triumph.

(Optional repeat from *)

SOLO
O clap your hands, your hands

ALL
O clap your hands.

47L
Psalm 47.1–9
© Editor/Jubilate Hymns

Clap your hands, all you nations:
shout to God with cries of joy.

How awesome is the Lord most high:
A **the King who rules
the whole wide earth!**

God has ascended to his throne:
B **with shouts of joy
and sound of trumpets.**

Sing praises to our God, sing praises:
A **sing praises to our King, sing praises.**

For God is King of all the earth:
B **sing to him a psalm of praise.**

God is seated on his throne:
A **he rules the nations of the world.**

The leaders of the nations come:
B **as subjects of our holy God.**

The lords of earth belong to God:
ALL **he reigns supreme. Amen.**

The congregation may divide at A and B.

48A
From Psalm 48
© Christopher Idle/Jubilate Hymns

1 Great is the Lord! His praise is great
on Zion's mount, his holy place;
the royal city crowns the earth
and shines on all with radiant grace.

2 God is the Tower
whose strength was shown
when Satan's armies threatened harm;
they gathered round, and looked, and ran
like boats before the driving storm.

3 Our ears have heard, our eyes have seen
what God the Lord of Hosts has done;
within these walls we celebrate
his steadfast love, his ageless throne.

4 God is the Judge whose mighty name
across the world with praise shall ring:
for his resplendent victories
let Zion shout and Judah sing!

5 God is the King whose kingdom's power
we see built up on every side;
we tell our children of our God
who will for ever be our Guide.

48B
From Psalm 48
© Richard Bewes/Jubilate Hymns

1 How great is God almighty
and how worthy to be praised,
for the city of our holy God
shall make the world amazed;
his mountain ever beautiful
before our vision raised –
the Joy of all the earth!
Glory be to God the Father,
glory be to God the Saviour,
glory to the Holy Spirit,
for ever, Three-in-One!

2 In Zion city God himself
will be our sure defence –
all the kings of earth who ever reigned
are stripped of vain pretence;
they see his throne in glory
and in fear they scatter thence –
the Power of all the earth!
Glory be to God . . .

3 Like eastward wind your mighty arm
will sweep your foes away;
we have seen fulfilled in Zion
all the truth of what you say:
we think of your eternal love
and worship every day
the Praise of all the earth!
Glory be to God . . .

4 The day shall come at last
when every wrong is turned to right;
we shall see in Zion's citadel
the ending of the night:
in every generation
we are passing on his light –
the God of all the earth!
Glory be to God . . .

48C
From Psalm 48, Steve McEwan
© 1985 Friends First Music/Word Music (UK)

Great is the Lord
and most worthy of praise:
the city of our God,
the holy place,
the joy of the whole earth.

Great is the Lord
in whom we have the victory;
he aids us against the enemy,
we bow down on our knees.

And, Lord,
    we want to lift your name on high,
and, Lord, we want to thank you
for the works you've done in our lives.
And, Lord,
    we trust in your unfailing love –
for you alone are God eternal
throughout earth and heaven above.

49A

From Psalm 49
© Paul Wigmore/Jubilate Hymns

1 What riches on this earth
   can buy one human breath?
   No wealth brings immortality,
   no treasure hinders death.

2 What wisdom in this life
   can know the mind of God?
   No sage can tread the paths of thought
   where our Creator trod.

3 What riches come from God
   when his desire is mine;
   his will unlocks a treasury,
   his love reveals a shrine!

4 And wisdom I shall know
   when he redeems my soul;
   for at his throne the mortal mind
   is sanctified and whole.

49B

From Psalm 49
© Michael Perry/Jubilate Hymns

1 O people, listen –
    hear God's wisdom crying!
   Although the darkness
    comes to rich and poor,
   and nothing mortal
    can survive our dying,
   yet in the morning
    justice shall endure:

2 For God will take the holy
    into heaven,
   by grace redeem the faithful
    from the grave;
   we leave behind us
    all this world has given,
   and trust God's mighty power
    to love and save!

3 To Father, Son and Spirit
    be the glory!
   Come, worship and adore
    the holy Name;
   let wisdom think upon
    our human story,
   and faith our ever-living God
    proclaim.

50A

From Psalm 50
© David Mowbray/Jubilate Hymns

1 Let God, who called the worlds to be,
   arise in all-consuming fire
   to judge the people righteously,
   and faithless ones with awe inspire.

2 This God is ours, and yet we break
   the covenant made long ago;
   God's words we foolishly forsake,
   God's ways we have refused to know.

3 For though our lips
    have preached God's law,
   our erring hearts have scorned the Name;
   we choose the thief and slanderer
   as friends, and so increase our shame.

4 What then shall God the Lord demand?
   Not gifts or lavish offering,
   but vows and promises performed,
   and lives from which true praises spring!

50B

From Psalm 50
© Michael Perry/Jubilate Hymns

1 God speaks – the Lord of all the earth,
   and calls the world to hear:
   what glory shines,
    what light springs forth,
   to draw the people near!

   Says God, the righteous one, the wise,
   'Your worship I decline;
   I have no need of sacrifice
   for all the world is mine.'

2 'Yet honour me, fulfil your vow,
   in truth prepare the road –
   so to the faithful I will show
   the saving grace of God.'

   Then lift your hearts and voices high
   to Father and to Son
   and Spirit – Three in majesty,
   our God for ever One!

51A
From Psalm 51 adapted from *The Psalter* 1912
© in this version Word & Music/Jubilate Hymns

1 God, be merciful to me,
   let your love my refuge be;
   my offences wash away,
   cleanse me from my sin today.
   My transgressions I confess,
   grief and guilt my soul oppress;
   I have sinned against your grace
   and provoked you to your face.

2 Wash me, wash me pure within,
   cleanse, O cleanse me from my sin:
   in your righteousness I trust,
   in your judgements you are just.
   Come, salvation to impart,
   teach your wisdom to my heart;
   make me pure, your grace bestow,
   that your mercy I may know.

3 Gracious God, my heart renew,
   make my spirit right and true;
   from my sins O hide your face,
   blot them out in boundless grace.
   Cast your servant not away,
   let your Spirit with me stay;
   make me joyful, willing, strong,
   teach me your salvation's song!

51B
From Psalm 51, © David Frost
Pointing © Wm Collins

Have mercy on me O God in your
en'during ' goodness:
according to
   the fulness of your compassion * '
blot out ' my of'fences.
Wash me thoroughly ' from my '
wickedness:
and ' cleanse me ' from my ' sin.

For I acknowledge ' my re'bellion:
and my ' sin is ' ever · be'fore me.
Against you only have I sinned * and
done what is evil ' in your ' eyes:
so you will be just in your sentence *
and ' blameless ' in your ' judging.

Purge me with hyssop and I ' shall be '
clean:
wash me
and I ' shall be ' whiter · than ' snow.
Create in me a clean ' heart O ' God:
and re'new a · right ' spirit · with'in me.

Do not cast me ' out · from your '
presence:
do not take your ' holy ' spirit '
   from me.
O give me the gladness of your ' help
a'gain:
and sup'port me ·
with a ' willing ' spirit.

You take no pleasure in sacrifice or ' I
would ' give it:
burnt ' offerings · you ' do not ' want.
The sacrifice of God is a ' broken ' spirit:
a broken and contrite heart O God '
you will ' not de'spise.

Glory to the Father and ' to the ' Son:
and ' to the ' Holy ' Spirit;
as it was in the be'ginning · is ' now:
and shall be for ' ever. ' A'men.

51C
From Psalm 51
© Jonathan Barnes

1 Have mercy, Lord, as you promise,
   wash me and cleanse me from my guilt:
   for I can see the wrong in my life;
   against you, Lord, have I sinned.

2 Your sentence on me is righteous,
   for I have sinned since my beginning;
   and, Lord, you look for truth in my heart –
   so teach me wisdom, I pray.

3 Lord, wash me from my uncleanness,
   fill me with joy where once was sadness;
   give me a heart renewed, O my Lord,
   your holy spirit within.

4 Turn from my sins and destroy them
   but let me never be forsaken;
   O give me joy in knowing you save,
   and make me love your command.

5 Lord, take my lips: I will praise you!
   No sacrifice I bring redeems me;
   all you require is my broken heart –
   a gift you will not refuse.

6 Lord, give your peace to your servant,
   protect and stay by me for ever;
   through your great love
      accept what I give,
   and fill my life with your praise!

51L

Psalm 51.6–12, and Psalm 143.6–10
© Editor/Jubilate Hymns

O Lord, I spread my hands out to you:
A **I thirst for you like dry ground.**

Teach me to do your will, for you are my
God:
B **let your good Spirit lead me in safety.**

You require sincerity and truth in me:
A **fill my mind with your wisdom.**

Create in me a pure heart, O God:
B **renew a faithful spirit in me.**

Do not cast me from your presence:
A **or take your Holy Spirit from me.**

Give me again the joy of your salvation:
B **and make me willing to obey.**

**Glory to the Father, and to the Son,
and to the Holy Spirit:
as it was in the beginning, is now,
and shall be for ever. Amen.**

The congregation may divide at A *and* B, *in
which case the* Gloria *should be used.
Psalms 51 and 143 have been grouped
together to provide for an occasion when the
person and work of the Holy Spirit is being
considered.*

52

From Psalm 52
© Paul Wigmore/Jubilate Hymns

1 Why in the dawning
    of another day
  does evil pierce the beauty
    we would see;
  when from the never-failing
    grace of God
  comes strength
    to make us flourish like a tree?

2 Why through the glory
    of another day
  comes razor-sharp the tongue
    that would destroy;
  when God,
    who at a word made all the earth,
  would be our certain stronghold
    and our joy?

3 Why at the evening
    of another day
  should boasting pride
    debase the good and pure;
  when God himself has blessed
    the contrite heart
  and blessing,
    made the soul's redemption sure?

4 O God, cast out the sin
    that kills the soul,
  that brings your whole creation
    into shame:
  and I through brightest day
    and darkest night
  with all the saints will praise
    your holy name!

53

From Psalm 53
© Michael Perry/Jubilate Hymns

1 Only the fool will say
    'There is no God';
  only the one whose way
    is full of lies:
  and God looks down in vain
    to see their love,
  for only few remain
    who do God's will.

2 Only from Zion shall
    salvation come;
  only in God we all
    may live in peace:
  lift high your voices, sing
    God's worthy praise,
  and only serve your king
    who stoops to save.

54

From Psalm 54
© Michael Perry/Jubilate Hymns

1 Save me, O God, hear my prayer,
  open your ears to my cry;
  keep me when evils prevail,
  strengthen my hand from on high.

2 Yet shall the Lord be my help –
  strong is the one who sustains;
  offerings of love I will bring
  God who eternally reigns!

55

From Psalm 55
© David Mowbray/Jubilate Hymns

1 O for the wings to fly afar
  and like a dove to rest,
  to live untroubled by the care
  which brings us to the test.

2 Of all my pain, the deepest wound
  was dealt not by some foe,
  but by my own familiar friend
  with whom I loved to go.

3 God, take this burden that I bring,
  and help me to forgive;
  then with a lighter heart, I'll sing
  and to your glory live!

56A
From Psalm 56
© Paul Wigmore/Jubilee Hymns

1 Be merciful to me, O God –
for those who harm draw near;
they turn my words of good intent,
they fill my day with fear.

2 I fear the hurtful word of scorn,
I dread the mocking gaze,
the deed that comes of cruelty,
the hatred it betrays.

3 But when I am afraid, O God,
I'll put my trust in you:
if God immortal strengthens me,
what harm can mortals do?

4 My tears are gone – now lead me, Lord,
defend me in the strife:
for then in your great strength I'll walk
led by the Light of Life.

56B
From Psalm 56
© Michael Perry/Jubilate Hymns

1 When I'm afraid
I will trust in God,
when I'm afraid I will say,
'What can anyone do to me –
God is mine today?'

2 When I'm alone
I will ask God's help,
when I'm alone I will pray –
how can anyone spoil my peace,
I am God's today?

3 While I'm alive
I will tell God's praise,
while I'm alive I will sing:
who can any more come between
me and God my king?

57A
From Psalm 57
© Michael Perry/Jubilate Hymns

1 Be gracious to me, Lord,
and hold my spirit fast,
that I may shelter by your side
until the storm is past.

2 Though snares are set for me,
yet will I sleep in peace,
for I have asked the care of God
whose love shall never cease.

3 My soul, awake and sing,
God's boundless love recall;
exalt God's name above the skies,
God's glory over all!

57B
From Psalm 57, Brent Chambers
© 1977 Scripture in Song/Thankyou Music

I will give thanks to you,
O Lord, among the people;
I will sing praises to you
among the nations:
for your steadfast love is great,
is great to the heavens,
and your faithfulness,
your faithfulness to the clouds.
Be exalted, O God,
above the heavens;
let your glory be over all the earth:
be exalted, O God,
above the heavens;
let your glory be over all the earth!

I will give thanks to you . . .

Be exalted, O God,
above the heavens;
let your glory be over all the earth:
be exalted, O God,
above the heavens;
let your glory, let your glory,
let your glory be over all the earth!

60
From Psalm 60
© Michael Perry/Jubilate Hymns

1 We are a land divided,
unworthy of you, Lord,
and yet by your great mercy
our peace can be restored.

Though we invite your anger
and fail to do your will,
yet if we turn and fear you
your love can triumph still.

2 Our God is strong to save us
and tread the evil down,
to raise the cause of justice
and gain the victor's crown.

Sing glory to the Father,
bring worship to the Son,
adore the Holy Spirit:
praise God the Three-in-One!

61A
From Psalm 61, J E Seddon
© Mrs M Seddon/Jubilate Hymns

1 Listen to my prayer, Lord,
hear my humble cry:
when my heart is fainting,
to your throne I fly.

2 In earth's farthest corner
  you will hear my voice:
  set me on your rock, Lord,
  then I shall rejoice.

MEN

3 You have been my shelter
  when the foe was near,
  as a tower of refuge
  shielding me from fear.

WOMEN

4 I will rest for ever
  in your care and love,
  guarded and protected
  as by wings above.

ALL

5 All that I have promised,
  help me to fulfil;
  and in all who love you
  work your perfect will.

6 May your truth and mercy
  keep me all my days;
  let my words and actions
  be my songs of praise!

61B
From Psalm 61
© Paul Wigmore/Jubilate Hymns

1 O God, hear me calling
        and answer, I pray!
  No distance can silence
        the words that I say,
  no mountain, no ocean
        can hinder my prayer
  when deep is my sorrow
        and dark my despair.

2 When trouble comes near me
        and enemies taunt,
  Lord, you are the fortress
        no evil can daunt;
  and safe on the rock that is higher than I
  your strength is my hope
        as you answer my cry.

3 For Lord you have heard
        all the vows I have made –
  my thoughts and intentions
        when homage I paid;
  with all who have lived
        by the fear of your name,
  Lord, grant all my prayers
        as your praise I proclaim.

4 I long for the day
        when your dwelling is mine,
  your wings for a shelter,
        your presence a shrine;
  I praise you on earth
        for your mercy and grace:
  what blessings I'll sing
        when I look on your face!

61C
From Psalm 61
Author unknown

1 Hear my cry, O Lord,
  and listen to my prayer:
  from the ends of the earth
  will I cry out to you.
      And when my heart is overwhelmed,
      lead me to the Rock
      that is higher than I,
      that is higher than I.

2 For you have been a hiding-place for me,
  a high tower, Lord,
  against the enemy.
      And when my heart . . .

62A
From Psalm 62
© David Mowbray/Jubilate Hymns

1 Rest in God, our God most mighty –
  thanks and praise to him belong;
  from the Lord comes our salvation,
  he remains our strength and song.
      Silently
      none but he
      waits, our rock and shield to be.

2 Trust no more in doubtful riches,
  part with those who work deceit:
  God himself is our rewarder,
  throned upon his judgement seat.
      Mercy waits
      at his gates
      for each one who falsehood hates.

3 In the past the Lord has spoken
  through his prophets and the law,
  shining lantern for our journey,
  where no path was known before.
      Hope again!
      Fears are vain –
      God's renewing power is plain.

4 Glory be to God the Father,
  glory be to God the Son,
  glory be to God the Spirit –
  ever Three and ever One.
      Trust God still,
      do his will;
      hold to him through good and ill!

62B

From Psalm 62, Jacques Berthier
© Taizé/Wm Collins

ALL
My soul is at rest in God alone,
my salvation comes from him.

SOLO/CHOIR
1 In God is my safety and glory,
the rock of my strength.
ALL My soul is at rest . . .

SOLO/CHOIR
2 Take refuge in God, all you people,
trust him at all times.
ALL My soul is at rest . . .

SOLO/CHOIR
3 Pour out your hearts before him,
for God is our refuge.
ALL My soul is at rest . . .

62C

From Psalm 62, John Daniels
© 1984 Ears and Eyes Music Ltd/
Boosey & Hawkes Music Publishers Ltd

I rest in God alone,
from him comes my salvation;
my soul finds rest in him,
my fortress – I'll not be shaken.

1 My hope is in the Lord
my honour and strength;
my refuge is in him for ever,
my trust and all of my heart –
in him alone my soul finds rest.
I rest in God alone . . .

2 O trust in him, you people,
pour out your hearts;
for God is our refuge for ever,
my trust and all of my heart –
in him alone my soul finds rest.

63A

From Psalm 63
© Timothy Dudley-Smith

1 God is my great desire,
his face I seek the first;
to him my heart and soul aspire,
for him I thirst.
As one in desert lands,
whose very flesh is flame,
in burning love I lift my hands
and bless his name.

2 God is my true delight,
my richest feast his praise,
through silent watches of the night,
through all my days.
To him my spirit clings,
on him my soul is cast;
beneath the shadow of his wings
he holds me fast.

3 God is my strong defence
in every evil hour;
in him I face with confidence
the tempter's power.
I trust his mercy sure,
with truth and triumph crowned:
my hope and joy for evermore
in him are found.

63B

From Psalm 63
© Paul Wigmore/Jubilate Hymns

1 O God, you are my God:
I seek you with my heart;
my soul is thirsty for you in a dry
and weary desert.

2 O God, you are my God:
your glory I have seen;
with singing shall my lips adore you,
Lord,
and glory give you.

3 O God, you are my God:
I think of you at night;
within the shadow of your wings I stay,
and you defend me.

4 O God, you are my God:
the victory is yours;
all evil by your justice overthrown
in holy anger.

5 As long as I shall live
my lips will sing your praise;
my hungry soul will feast upon your love,
and glorify you.

63C

From Psalm 63
© Basil Bridge

1 I seek you, Lord God, I yearn for you;
with longing my soul cries out for you
as the parched earth thirsts for rain.

2 In worship I come to seek your face:
O show me your glory and your grace –
let that vision quicken me.

3 The blessing of your unchanging love
I treasure all earthly good above:
let my voice declare your praise.

4 I'll praise you as long as life shall last;
   your mercy provides a rich repast,
      and my soul is satisfied.

5 In quiet my spirit shall recall
   your mercies so great to each and all –
      I am safe within your care.

63D
From Psalm 63, Phil Potter
© 1981 Thankyou Music

1 Because your love is better than life,
      with my lips I will glorify you;
      I will praise you as long as I live –
      in your name I lift my hands.

2 Because your Son has given me life,
      with my lips . . .

3 Because your Spirit is filling my life,
      with my lips . . .

4 Because your love is better than life,
      with my lips . . .

63E
From Psalm 63, Hugh Mitchell
© 1956, 1962 Singspiration Inc/MPI Ltd

1 Your loving-kindness is better than life,
   your loving-kindness is better than life;
      my lips shall praise you –
         so will I bless you;
   your loving-kindness is better than life.

2 I lift my hands up unto your name,
   I lift my hands up unto your name:
      my lips shall praise you,
         so will I bless you;
   your loving-kindness is better than life.

65A
From Psalm 65
© David Mowbray/Jubilate Hymns

1 God whose praise is sung in Zion,
   Lord who calls the worlds to be;
   maker of the mountain ranges,
   master of the roaring sea:
   we, with saints of every nation,
   sing your praise, who sets us free.

2 Visit, Lord, the earth to bless it,
   prosper all the growing corn;
   let the valleys fill with laughter
   and the lambs be safely born;
   crown the farmer's year with goodness,
   till the days of plenty dawn!

3 Glory be to God the Father,
   glory be to God the Son,
   Glory be to God the Spirit,
   ever Three and ever One!
   Earth's creator, Lord, life-giver,
   let your work through us be done!

65B
From Psalm 65, © David Frost
Pointing © Wm Collins

You are to be praised O ' God in ' Zion:
to you shall vows be paid '
you that ' answer ' prayer.
Those who dwell at the ends of the earth
are a'fraid at · your ' wonders:
the dawn and the ' evening '
   sing your ' praises.

You tend the ' earth and ' water it:
you ' make it ' rich and ' fertile.
You crown the ' year · with your '
goodness:
and the tracks
   where you have ' passed '
drip with ' fatness.

The pastures of the ' wilderness · run '
over:
and the ' hills are ' girded · with ' joy.
The meadows are ' clothed with ' sheep:
and the valleys
   stand so thick with corn
they ' shout for ' joy and ' sing.

Glory to the Father and ' to the ' Son:
and ' to the ' Holy ' Spirit;
as it was in the be'ginning · is ' now:
and shall be for ' ever. ' A'men.

65C
From Psalm 65
© Michael Saward/Jubilate Hymns

1 The earth is yours, O God –
   you nourish it with rain;
   the streams and rivers overflow,
   the land bears seed again.

2 The soil is yours, O God –
   the shoots are moist with dew;
   and ripened by the burning sun
   the corn grows straight and true.

3 The hills are yours, O God –
   their grass is lush and green,
   providing pastures for the flocks
   which everywhere are seen.

4 The whole rich land is yours
   for fodder or for plough:
   and so, for rain, sun, soil and seed,
   O God, we thank you now!

65L
Psalm 65.1–13
© Editor/Jubilee Hymns

O God, it is right for us to praise you,
because you answer our prayers:

You care for the land and water it:
A **and make it rich and fertile.**

You fill the running streams with water:
B **and irrigate the land.**

You soften the ground with showers:
A **and make the young crops grow.**

You crown the year with goodness:
B **and give us a plentiful harvest.**

The pastures are filled with flocks:
A **the hillsides are clothed with joy.**

The fields are covered with grain:
ALL **they shout for joy and sing.**

**Glory to the Father, and to the Son,
and to the Holy Spirit:
as it was in the beginning, is now,
and shall be for ever. Amen.**

The congregation may divide at A *and* B.

66A
From Psalm 66
© Christopher Idle/Jubilee Hymns

1 Praise our God with shouts of joy,
 sing the glory of his name;
 join to lift his praises high,
 through the world his love proclaim.

2 Come and see what God has done
 by the power of his right hand;
 see the battles he has won
 by his word of swift command.

3 God has tamed the raging seas,
 carved a highway through the tide,
 paid the cost of our release,
 come himself to be our guide.

4 God has put us to the test,
 bringing us through flood and fire
 into freedom, peace, and rest,
 for our good is his desire.

5 He has not despised my prayer
 nor kept back his love from me;
 he has raised me from despair –
 to our God all glory be!

66B
From Psalm 66
© International Bible Society

1 Shout with joy to God, all the earth!
 Sing to the glory of his name
 and offer him praise and glory.
 Say to God,
    'How awesome are your deeds,
 how great your power over all –
 your enemies will fall down before you!'
   Come, let us rejoice in him,
   come, let us rejoice in him,
   come, let us rejoice in him,
   come, let us rejoice in him!

2 All the earth bows down to you,
 they sing their praise to you –
 praise to your name, to your name.
 Come and see what God has done,
 how awesome are his works for us:
 he turned the sea into dry land
 and they crossed over!
   Come, let us rejoice . . .

3 Praise our God, O peoples –
 let the sound of all his praise be heard:
 he has preserved our lives,
 our feet from slipping.
 As with silver, you refined us, Lord,
 put us through water and through fire,
 and brought us to a place of abundance.
   Come, let us rejoice . . .

4 Come and listen, all who fear the Lord,
 and let me tell what he has done:
 my praise was on my tongue
    as I cried to him;
 if I cherished sin within my heart,
 the Lord would not have heard my cry,
 but surely he has turned
    and he has listened.
   Come, let us rejoice . . .

5 If I cherished sin within my heart,
 the Lord would not have heard my cry,
 but surely he has turned
    and he has listened.
 He has heard my voice –
    praise be to God! –
 my prayer he has not turned away,
 and he has not withheld his love from me!
   Come, let us rejoice . . .

66L

Psalm 66.1–20
© Editor/Jubilee Hymns

Praise your God with shouts of joy:
all the earth, sing praise to him.

Sing the glory of his name:
A **offer him your highest praise.**

Say to him: How great you are:
B **wonderful the things you do!**

All your enemies bow down:
C **all the earth sings praise to you.**

Come and see what God has done:
A **causing mortal men to fear –**
B **for he turned the sea to land,**
C **let his people safely through.**

We rejoice at what he does –
A **ruling through eternity,**
B **watching over all the world,**
C **keeping every rebel down.**

Praise our God, you nations, praise:
A **let the sound of praise be heard!**
B **God sustains our very lives:**
C **keeps our feet along the way.**

Once, you tested us, O God –
A **silver purified by fire –**

Let us fall into a trap,
B **placed hard burdens on our backs –**

Sent us through the flame and flood:
C **now you bring us safely home.**

I will come to worship you:
A **bring to you my offering,**
B **give you what I said I would,**
C **when the troubles threatened me.**

All who love and honour God:
A **come and listen, while I tell**
B **what great things he did for me**
C **when I cried to him for help,**
A **when I praised him with my songs.**
B **When my heart was free from sin,**
C **then he listened to my prayer.**

Praise the Lord who heard my cry:
ALL **God has shown his love to me! Amen.**

The congregation may divide at A, B *and* C.

67A

From Psalm 67, *Deus miseratur*
© Timothy Dudley-Smith

1 Mercy, blessing, favour, grace,
saving power to us be shown;
brightness of the Father's face
to the nations now be known.

2 Shout in triumph, sing in praise!
Peoples all, proclaim his worth:
just and righteous are his ways,
sovereign Lord of all the earth.

3 Harvests year by year proclaim
blessings new in plenty poured;
all the earth shall fear his name,
all his people praise the Lord.

67B

From Psalm 67, *Deus miseratur*
© Stephen Horsfall/Jubilee Hymns

1 May God be gracious,
    may we see his face;
throughout the wide world
    may his power be known.
May all the nations
    trust his saving grace,
and come to worship,
and come to worship him
    before his throne.

2 He holds our future
    safe within his hand;
he judges rightly
    and he guides our ways.
Earth yields its increase –
    God will bless our land:
may all his people,
may all his people
    give him thanks and praise!

67C

Psalm 67, *Deus miseratur*
© David Frost, Pointing © Wm Collins

1 Let God be gracious to ˈ us and ˈ bless us:
and make his ˈ face ˈ shine upˈon us,
2 that your ways may be ˈ known on ˈ earth:
your liberating ˈ power ·
aˈmong all ˈ nations.

3 Let the peoples ˈ praise you · O ˈ God:
let ˈ all the ˈ peoples ˈ praise you.
4 Let the nations be ˈ glad and ˈ sing:
for you judge the peoples with integrity *
and govern the ˈ nations · upˈon ˈ earth.

5 Let the peoples ˈ praise you · O ˈ God:
let ˈ all the ˈ peoples ˈ praise you.
6 Then the earth will ˈ yield its ˈ fruitfulness:
and ˈ God our ˈ God will ˈ bless us.

Second part
7 God ˈ shall ˈ bless us:
and all the ˈ ends · of the ˈ earth
    will ˈ fear him.

Glory to the Father and ˈ to the ˈ Son:
and ˈ to the ˈ Holy ˈ Spirit;
as it was in the beˈginning · is ˈ now:
and shall be for ˈ ever. ˈ Aˈmen.

67D

From Psalm 67, Phil Potter
© 1986 Ears and Eyes Music Ltd/
Boosey & Hawkes Music Publishers Ltd

May God be gracious to us and bless us,
and make his face shine upon us;
may God be gracious to us and bless us,
and make his face shine upon us.

67E

From Psalm 67, Chris Rolinson
© 1988 Thankyou Music

ALL   Let the people praise you, O God,
MEN   let all the people praise you,
WOMEN   let all the people praise you.
ALL   Let the people praise you, O God,
MEN   let all the people praise you,
WOMEN   let all the people praise you,
ALL   let all the people praise you.

1 May your ways be known on earth,
and your power to save us:
then the peoples of the world
shall fear you, shall fear you.
    Let the people . . .

2 We'll be glad and sing for joy,
for you rule with justice;
then the ends of all the earth
shall fear you, shall fear you.
    Let the people . . .

3 For you are a gracious God,
we delight to praise you:
then our land shall see
the fruits of blessing, your blessing.
    Let the people . . .

67L

Psalm 67.1–7
© Editor/Jubilate Hymns

May God be gracious to us and bless us:
A **and make his face to shine upon us.**

Let your ways be known upon earth:
B **your saving grace to every nation.**

Let the peoples praise you, O God:
ALL **let the peoples praise you.**

Let the nations be glad:
A **and sing aloud for joy.**

Because you judge the peoples justly:
B **and guide the nations of the earth.**

Let the peoples praise you, O God:
ALL **let the peoples praise you.**

Then the land will yield its harvest:
A **and God, our God, will bless us.**

God will bless us:
B **and people will fear him**
ALL **to the ends of the earth. Amen.**

**Glory to the Father, and to the Son,
and to the Holy Spirit:
as it was in the beginning, is now,
and shall be for ever. Amen.**

The congregation may divide at A *and* B.

68A

From Psalm 68
© Christopher Idle/Jubilate Hymns

ALL
1 Let God arise! his enemies be gone
    and melt like wax before the holy One.

WOMEN
2 Make known the Lord,
       and sound his name aloud
    to praise the king
       who rides upon the cloud.

MEN
3 Father and judge,
       he gave the world his law
    with freedom, love and justice
       for the poor.

WOMEN
4 God marched ahead,
       strong shepherd of his flock;
    the heavens opened;
       earth in terror shook.

MEN
5 God spoke the word,
       and faithful was the band
    of those who took his truth to every land.

ALL
6 See God ascend,
       with captives as his prize,
    and gifts for all who shall in him arise.

WOMEN
7 Bless day by day
       the living God who saves,
    who raises up his people
       from their graves.

MEN
8 Draw near his throne:
       musicians lead our song!
    all nations, tribes, and races
       join the throng.

WOMEN
9 All strength is his!
       the rebels reign no more;
    he scatters all who take delight in war.

MEN
10 God rules on high,
        and mighty is his voice:
    to God be praise;
        in God we shall rejoice.

ALL
11 Glory to God, creator, saviour, friend
    whose greatness, love, and wisdom
        never end.

68B From Psalm 68, Graham Kendrick
© 1984 Make Way Music/Thankyou Music

    Let God arise,
    and let his enemies be scattered,
    and let those who hate him
    flee before him;
    let God arise,
    and let his enemies be scattered,
    and let those who hate him
    flee away.

MEN
    But let the righteous be glad;
    let them exult before God,
    let them rejoice with gladness,
    building up a highway for the king.
    We go in the name of the Lord:
    let us shout,
    'Go up in the name of the Lord!'

WOMEN
    . . . the righteous be glad,
    let them exult before God;
    O let them rejoice
    for the king;
    let us shout,
    'Go up in the name of the Lord!'

69A From Psalm 69
© Michael Perry/Jubilate Hymns

1 When the waters cover me,
       save me, O God;
   when I look and cannot see,
   when I seek what cannot be,
   when my friends abandon me,
       save me, O God.

2 You know all my guilty fears,
       thank you, O God,
   you have heard with open ears,
   you have seen my contrite tears,
   you will bless me all the years,
       thank you, O God.

69B From Psalm 69
© Michael Perry/Jubilate Hymns

1 When my sorrows cover me,
       save me, O God;
   when my friends abandon me,
   when I seek what cannot be,
   when I look and cannot see,
       (save me, O God,)
   save me, O God.

2 You know all my guilty fears,
       thank you, O God;
   you have heard with open ears,
   you have seen my contrite tears,
   you will bless my future years,
       (thank you, O God,
       thank you, O God,)
   thank you, O God.

70 From Psalm 70, Bert Polman
© 1987 CRC Publications

1 Come quickly, Lord, to rescue me,
   and hasten to my help, I pray.
   May all who seek to take my life
   be put to shame without delay.

2 May all who seek your name rejoice,
   your praise in gratitude record.
   May those who love your saving power
   say evermore, 'Exalt the Lord!'

3 Yet I am poor and needy, Lord:
   be quick to hear my urgent plea.
   You are my help, my Saviour God!
   Do not delay; remember me.

71A From Psalm 71
© Michael Perry/Jubilate Hymns

1 From time beyond my memory
   your love has been my rock, O Lord;
   since childhood days I trusted you,
   and in my youth declared your word.

2 But when the years are passing by
   as friends depart and spirits fail:
   O God, come quickly to my side,
   that in your strength I may prevail.

3 We praise you, God, the holy One,
   proclaim your love from day to day;
   exalt your triumphs to the skies
   and trust your mercy come what may:

4 Sing glory to the Father, Son –
   and to the Spirit glory be;
   let psalms to God on earth begun
   resound through all eternity!

71B
From Psalm 71
© International Bible Society

I will praise you with the harp
for your faithfulness, O my God;
I will sing my praise to you
with the lyre, with the lyre.
    O Holy One of Israel,
    O Holy One of Israel,
    O Holy One of Israel:
    my lips will shout for joy,
    my lips will shout for joy,
    when I sing my praise to you,
    when I sing my praise to you,
    when I sing my praise to you –
    for I have been redeemed,
    for I have been redeemed!
    I'll speak of all your righteous acts,
    I'll speak of all your righteous acts,
    I'll speak of all your righteous acts,
    and tell it all day long,
    and tell it all day long.

I will praise you with the harp
for your faithfulness, O my God;
I will sing my praise to you
with the lyre, with the lyre.

Those who want to harm me
are put to shame and confused;
I will sing my praise to you
with the lyre, with the lyre.
    I've been redeemed . . .

72
From Psalm 72
© Michael Perry/Jubilate Hymns

1 To those who rule our land,
    give justice, love and truth;
    so help them to defend the poor,
    to keep us safe, to guard the law,
    and prosper at your hand:

2 Let mercy all their days
    fall as refreshing showers;
    so guide the people with your light
    that we may flourish in your sight,
    and earth be filled with praise!

73
From Psalm 73
© Michael Perry/Jubilate Hymns

1 Surely God the Lord is good,
    guiding all whose hearts are pure;
    at God's hands we take our food,
    in God's love we are secure:
    vainly do the heathen cry,
    'Can the Most High watch us all?'
    Shamed by that all-seeing eye
    soon the boasting proud will fall.

2 When my stumbling footsteps tire,
    strengthen me in all I do –
    earth has no more I desire;
    whom have I in heaven but you?
    Though my flesh and heart shall fail,
    you supply immortal needs;
    with your help I shall prevail
    and proclaim your perfect deeds.

3 Yes, this earth-bound fantasy
    shall disperse when you arise;
    when you come to welcome me
    to your home beyond the skies.
    Glory be to God today,
    every heart by grace forgiven;
    souls redeemed and angels say,
    Glory in the highest heaven!

75
From Psalm 75
© Michael Perry/Jubilate Hymns

1 O God, we thank you that your name
    is known and feared through all the earth,
    your sentence waits the appointed time
    and thunder
            brings your judgements forth.

2 The proud you caution not to boast,
    the wicked, not to raise their eyes;
    for you are king from east to west,
    and you alone shall have the praise!

3 We come before you, God of gods –
    your power shall cut the wicked down;
    we worship you as Lord of lords –
    you lift us up to share your throne!

76
From Psalm 76
© David Mowbray/Jubilate Hymns

1 Silent the earth when God arose
    in justice for the meek,
    when all the strong were cast aside
    and mercy spared the weak.

2 So let earth's tyrants gaze in fear,
    as evil-doers should,
    to see their wicked deeds transformed
    to providential good.

3 Let God be praised, Jerusalem,
    and known throughout the earth:
    now is the moment, now the time
    to tell God's sovereign worth!

77
From Psalm 77
© Michael Perry/Jubilate Hymns

1 I cried out for heaven to hear me,
    I reached out in sorrow for help;
    no counsel or comfort would cheer me,
    my spirit abandoned all hope.

2 But in my despair I remembered
the songs of a long time ago,
and dreamed of the majesty splendoured
of God the almighty, the true:

3 You spoke in the wind and the thunder,
the earth and the elements shook;
your power tore the waters asunder,
as Shepherd, you guided your flock.

4 Then thank you, O God, for your merit,
your faithfulness always the same;
the Father, the Son and the Spirit –
one Lord over all. Praise your name!

78
From Psalm 78
© Michael Perry/Jubilate Hymns

1 We will tell each generation
all that you, our God, have done;
how you called and led our nation,
chose us out to be your own:

2 Tell the times of our rebelling –
how we wandered from your way,
how your law our love compelling
taught us humbly to obey:

3 Tell how once, when spite and terror
threatened to engulf our land,
you defended us with vigour,
saved us by a mighty hand.

4 Tell the grace that falls from heaven,
angels' food as faith's reward;
tell how sins may be forgiven
through the mercy of the Lord.

80
From Psalm 80
© David Mowbray/Jubilate Hymns

1 God of hosts, you chose a vine
meant to bear the finest wine,
set it in a promised land,
nurtured by your careful hand:

2 Like a cedar, it grew strong –
deep its roots, its tendrils long;
yet, in envy those around
stripped its branches to the ground.

3 Desolate, to God we cry:
'Spare us from the enemy!'
God of hosts, turn back again,
all such wickedness restrain:

4 Turn us too, for we have failed,
faithfulness has not prevailed;
visit, Lord, and heal your vine,
on its fruit let glory shine!

80L
Psalm 80.1–19
© Editor/Jubilate Hymns

A Hear us, O Shepherd of Israel, leader of
your flock.

B Hear us from your throne above the
cherubim.

C Shine forth, awaken your strength, and
come to save us.
**Bring us back, O God, and save us,
make your face to shine upon us.**

A O Lord God almighty, how long will you
be angry with your people's prayers?

B You have given us sorrow to eat and
tears to drink.

C You have made us a source of contention
to our neighbours, and our enemies
insult us.
**Bring us back, O God, and save us,
make your face to shine upon us.**

A Return to us, O God Almighty, look down
from your heaven and see.

B Look on this vine that you planted with
your own hand, this child you raised for
yourself.

C Let your hand rest upon the people you
have chosen, then we will not turn away
from you; revive us, and we shall praise
your name.
**Bring us back, O God, and save us,
make your face to shine upon us.**

**Glory to the Father, and to the Son,
and to the Holy Spirit:
as it was in the beginning, is now,
and shall be for ever. Amen.**

Ministers/leaders may divide at A, B *and* C.

81
From Psalm 81
© David Mowbray/Jubilate Hymns

1 Sing merrily to God
whose arm has done great things,
and play with all the skill you have
on trumpet, pipe and strings.

2 Remember Israel's plight
in Egypt's far-off land:
how God, unaided, rescued them
with strong and outstretched hand.

3 Remember too their pride,
their murmurings on the way;
recall how they forsook the Lord
and chose to disobey.

4 Let us not act like them,
  but walk in faith again
  and claim the gifts that God will shower
  refreshing as the rain.

5 Sing merrily to God,
  the Shepherd of his flock
  who feeds his people, as of old,
  with honey from the rock.

82 From Psalm 82
© Michael Perry/Jubilate Hymns

1 God is king – be warned, you mighty;
  God is judge through all the land:
  order your affairs with justice,
  rule with firm but gentle hand.

  Help the weak, support the needy,
  take to heart the fatherless;
  prove the rights of those who suffer,
  meet the poor in their distress.

2 There are lands that have no honour,
  hear no wisdom, see no light;
  blind, they stumble in the darkness,
  leaderless, they shake with fright.

  Tremble, all you mighty rulers;
  every nation, know God's worth:
  power and wealth are God's possession,
  who alone shall judge the earth!

84A From Psalm 84
© Barbara Woollett/Jubilate Hymns

1 How lovely is your dwelling-place,
  O Lord most high,
  we long to know more of your grace,
  and yearn to see you face to face,
  O Lord most high!

2 The sparrow comes to build her nest,
  O Lord most high,
  and in your house finds peace and rest:
  so may we too be ever blessed,
  O Lord most high!

3 Your people come to you again,
  O Lord most high,
  for here we feel your strength, like rain
  refreshing us through toil and pain,
  O Lord most high!

4 In fellowship your love we share,
  O Lord most high;
  far better is one day of prayer
  than any spent in worldly care,
  O Lord most high!

5 How lovely is your dwelling-place,
  O Lord most high;
  we bring you all our trust and praise,
  and ask your blessing on our days,
  O Lord most high!

84B From Psalm 84
© Paul Wigmore/Jubilate Hymns

1 O Lord, the mansions where you dwell
  are overflowing with your love;
  while here on earth my soul knows well
  of lasting joy in heaven above.

2 And, Lord, my heart and flesh cry out
  in longing for that holy place;
  an end to sorrow, sin and doubt,
  the revelation of your face.

3 One day within your courts, O Lord,
  one day set free from every fear,
  one day with your dear name adored
  is better than a thousand here.

4 For those, O Lord, who trust in you:
  direct their eyes to see your ways,
  their heart to love, their hands to do,
  their head to bow, their lips to praise.

84C Psalm 84, © David Frost
Pointing © Wm Collins

1 **How lovely ' is your ' dwelling-place:**
  O ' Lord ' God of ' hosts!
2 My soul has a desire and longing to
  enter the ' courts · of the ' Lord:
  my heart and my flesh re'joice ·
  in the ' living ' God.
3 The sparrow has found her a home *
  and the swallow a nest where she may '
  lay her ' young:
  even your altar * O Lord of ' hosts '
  my ' King · and my ' God.
4 Blessed are those who ' dwell in · your '
  house:
  they will ' always · be ' praising ' you.
5 Blessed are those whose ' strength ·
  is in ' you:
  in whose ' heart ·
  are the ' highways · to ' Zion;
6 who going through the valley of dryness
  find there a spring from ' which to '
  drink:
  till the autumn ' rain
  shall ' clothe it · with ' blessings.

Second part
7 They go from ' strength to ' strength:
  they appear every one of them
  before the ' God of ' gods in ' Zion.

8 O Lord God of hosts ' hear my ' prayer:
   give ' ear O ' God of ' Jacob.
9 Behold O God ' him who · reigns ' over
   us:
   and look upon
   the ' face of ' your a'nointed.

10 One day in your courts is ' better · than
   a ' thousand:
   I would rather stand at the threshold
     of the house of my God *
   than ' dwell ·
     in the ' tents of · un'godliness.
11 For the Lord God is a rampart and a
   shield *
   the Lord gives ' favour · and ' honour:
   and no good thing will he withhold
   from ' those who ' walk in ' innocence.

Second part
12 O Lord ' God of ' hosts:
   blessed are those
   who ' put their ' trust in ' you.

   Glory to the Father and ' to the ' Son:
   and ' to the ' Holy ' Spirit;
   as it was in the be'ginning · is ' now:
   and shall be for ' ever. ' A'men.

84D
From Psalm 84, Tom Howard
© 1982 Maranatha! Music/Word Music (UK)

1 How lovely is your dwelling-place,
   almighty Lord!
   There's a hunger deep
   inside my soul:
   only in your presence
   are my heart and flesh restored –
   how lovely.
     How lovely is your dwelling-place,
     almighty Lord!
     There's a hunger
     deep inside my soul:
     only in your presence
     are my heart and flesh restored –
     how lovely is your dwelling-place.

2 In your courts there's shelter
   for the greatest and the small;
   the sparrow has a place to build her nest,
   the pilgrim finds refreshment
     in the rains that fall;
   and each one has the strength
   to meet the test.
     How lovely . . .

3 A single day is better
   when spent in humble praise,
   than a thousand days of living
     without you:
   the Lord bestows his favour
   on each one who obeys
   and blessings on the one
     whose heart is true.
     How lovely . . .

84E
From Psalm 84, Jonathan Asprey
© 1975 Celebration/Thankyou Music

1 How lovely is your dwelling-place,
   O Lord of hosts, to me.
   My soul is longing and fainting
   the courts of the Lord to see;
   my heart and flesh, they are singing
   for joy to the living God:
   how lovely is your dwelling-place,
     O Lord of hosts, to me!

2 Even the sparrow finds a home
   where he can settle down;
   and the swallow, she can build a nest
   where she may lay her young
   within the courts of the Lord of hosts,
   my king, my Lord, and my God:
   and happy are those
     who are dwelling where
     the song of praise is sung!

3 And I'd rather be a door-keeper
   and only stay a day,
   than live the life of a sinner
   and have to stay away;
   for the Lord is shining as the sun,
   and the Lord, he's like a shield –
   and no good thing does he withhold
   from those who walk his way.

4 How lovely . . .

85A
From Psalm 85
© Christopher Idle/Jubilate Hymns

1 When this land knew
       God's gracious love outpoured
   guilt was removed
       and captive lives restored;
   then was drawn back
       the anger of the Lord,
   his people pardoned, their sins forgiven.

2 But now where wrong
       so flagrantly has trod
   will you for ever punish with your rod?
   Once more revive us!
       Give us life, O God!
   Give joy for anguish; for wrath, salvation.

3 O let me hear
      God's word of sweet command:
   peace to his saints, salvation is at hand;
   peace to his people, glory in our land
   for those who fear him,
         who turn and worship.

4 That day draws near
      when truth will join with grace,
   justice and peace will meet
      in love's embrace;
   faith on the earth, and from his holy place
   he comes in glory, the righteous Saviour.

85B From Psalm 85, Jacques Berthier
© 1982, 1983 and 1984 Taizé/ Wm Collins

CONTINUOUS RESPONSE — ALL
      Grant to us your peace, Lord
      grant to us . . .
   OR:
      Dona nobis pacem,
      dona nobis pacem.

VERSES — SOLO
1 I will hear what the Lord has to say –
   a voice that speaks of peace;
   peace for his people
         and peace for his friends,
   and peace for those
         who turn to him in their hearts.

2 His help is near for those who adore him,
   his glory will dwell in our land.

3 Mercy and faithfulness have met,
   justice and peace have embraced;
   faithfulness shall spring from the earth,
   and justice look down from heaven.

4 The Lord will grant us his joy,
   and our earth shall yield its fruit;
   justice shall walk before him,
   and peace shall follow his steps.

86A From Psalm 86
© Michael Perry/Jubilee Hymns

1 Hear me, O Lord,
      and respond to my prayer,
   guard well my life, for I love you:
   nothing compares
      with the wonders you do,
   for there is no god above you.

2 Bring me your joy as I worship you, Lord,
   come to my heart, for I need you;
   teach me your way,
      let me walk in your truth –
   I cannot fail when I heed you.

3 Give me a sign of your goodness,
      O Lord,
   grant me the strength that obeys you:
   you are compassion, abounding in love,
   you are my king, and I praise you!

86B From Psalm 86, John Daniels
© 1986 Thankyou Music

   Teach me your way, O Lord,
   and I will walk in your truth;
   give me an undivided heart
   that I may fear your name.

   And I will praise you, O Lord my God,
   with all of my heart;
   and I will praise you, O Lord my God,
   and I will glorify your name for ever.

   Teach me your way . . .

87 From Psalm 87
© David Mowbray/Jubilate Hymns

1 For all your boundless gifts
   we offer, Lord, our praise;
   for places which have sheltered us
   and shaped our earthly days.

2 So was Jerusalem
   both Israel's joy and pride,
   the city of the Lord most high
   where kings were born and died.

3 Through all our cities, Lord,
   let streams of justice flow;
   there may the kingdom of your Christ –
   a spreading cedar – grow.

4 So trumpeters shall sound
   and earth and heaven ring;
   then shall the people say Amen
   and songs of gladness sing!

88 From Psalm 88
© Michael Perry/Jubilate Hymns

1 O Lord, the God who saves me,
   to you my spirit cries;
   my world is full of trouble,
   and hope of mercy dies.

2 Your anger lies upon me,
   I cannot make amends;
   your waves, they overwhelm me,
   you take away my friends.

3 And shall the dead sing praises,
   and can the darkness see
   your righteous ways, your wonders,
   your faithfulness to me?

4 I call to you in waking,
  and seek you all day long:
  O hear me, Lord and Saviour –
  restore to me my song.

5 My God shall yet uplift me,
  the Spirit come to save,
  and Jesus my redeemer
  shall tear me from the grave!

89A
From Psalm 89
© Timothy Dudley-Smith

1 Timeless love! We sing the story,
  praise his wonders, tell his worth;
  love more fair than heaven's glory,
  love more firm than ancient earth!
    Tell his faithfulness abroad:
    who is like him? Praise the Lord!

2 By his faithfulness surrounded,
  north and south his hand proclaim;
  earth and heaven formed and founded,
  skies and seas, declare his name!
    Wind and storm obey his word:
    who is like him? Praise the Lord!

3 Truth and righteousness enthrone him,
  just and equal are his ways;
  more than happy, those who own him,
  more than joy, their songs of praise!
    Sun and shield and great reward:
    who is like him? Praise the Lord!

89B
From Psalm 89, Richard Henderson
© 1987 Ears and Eyes Music Ltd/
Boosey & Hawkes Music Publishers Ltd

  I will sing of the Lord for ever,
  for his promises are good;
  I will sing of the Lord for ever,
  for his promises are good!

  His love never changes,
  he is always faithful –
  he will restore Jerusalem;
  his love never changes,
  he is always faithful –
  he will restore Jerusalem.
    I will sing . . .

90A
From Psalm 90
© Timothy Dudley-Smith

1 Our God eternal, reigning,
  creation's life sustaining,
    our refuge and our home;
  enthroned, in light surrounded,
  when earth was yet unfounded,
    the living God, to him we come.

2 We fade, a dream that passes,
  like withered meadow grasses
    when summer's sun has shone.
  Before that face all-seeing
  of God who gave us being
    we pass away and we are gone.

3 O God of mercy, hear us,
  in steadfast love draw near us,
    from age to age the same;
  that we, by grace defended,
  when earthly days are ended
    may live to praise a Saviour's name.

90B
From Psalm 90
© David Mowbray/Jubilate Hymns

1 God everlasting, at your word
  the hills in splendour rise;
  they overshadow human life
  whose glory swiftly dies.

2 Our days like dreams come to an end,
  our story soon is told –
  when strength is spent, and beauty fades,
  and bodies have grown old.

3 Teach us, good Lord, to count our days,
  to cherish every hour;
  to seek your will, to do your work,
  and trust your mighty power.

4 Lord, at your hand we have received
  the cup of joy and pain:
  pour out the fulness of your grace
  and we shall sing again!

90C
From Psalm 90
© Basil Bridge

1 O Lord, the refuge of each generation,
  you reigned before the universe began;
  we bear your stamp,
    the marks of your creation,
  and yet how frail we are,
    how brief life's span!

2 One thousand years
    like yesterday in passing,
  our fleeting lives
    like half-remembered dreams,
  or weeds that flower at noon
    but die by evening –
  so, Lord, to you
    our transient glory seems.

3 O Holy Lord, forgive our self-deceiving –
  our secret sins are clear before your face:
  grant us release,
    the joy of those believing
  they are restored by your eternal grace.

4 Time rushes on:
       give us a heart of wisdom
that seeks your will
       and follows your commands;
show us your deeds,
       your glory to our children,
work out your timeless purpose
       through our hands.

90D
From Psalm 90, collected J G Wagner
© in this version Word & Music/Jubilate Hymns

1 Lord, you have been our dwelling-place
through all the ages of our race;
before the mountains had their birth
or ever you had formed the earth,
from everlasting you are God,
to everlasting our abode.

2 O teach us all to count our days,
and set our hearts on wisdom's ways;
turn, Lord, to us in our distress,
in pity now your servants bless;
let mercy's dawn dispel our night,
and all our day with joy be bright.

3 O send the day of joy and light,
for long has been our sorrow's night!
Afflicted through the weary years,
we wait until your help appears:
O God be present at our side,
your name in us be glorified.

4 So let there be on us bestowed
the beauty of the Lord our God;
the work accomplished by our hand
be pleased to bless, and make it stand;
let all we do in deed or word,
endure to glorify our Lord!

91A
From Psalm 91
© Timothy Dudley-Smith

1 Safe in the shadow of the Lord,
beneath his hand and power,
    I trust in him,
    I trust in him,
my fortress and my tower.

2 My hope is set on God alone
though Satan spreads his snare;
    I trust in him,
    I trust in him
to keep me in his care.

MEN
3 From fears and phantoms of the night,
from foes about my way,
    I trust in him,
    I trust in him
by darkness as by day.

WOMEN
4 His holy angels keep my feet
secure from every stone;
    I trust in him,
    I trust in him,
and unafraid go on.

ALL
5 Strong in the everlasting name,
and in my Father's care,
    I trust in him,
    I trust in him,
who hears and answers prayer.

6 Safe in the shadow of the Lord,
possessed by love divine,
    I trust in him,
    I trust in him,
and meet his love with mine.

91B
From Psalm 91, Gail Cole and Glen Cummings
© 1975 Church of the Messiah

    I will dwell in his secret place,
    in his shadow I will abide;
    in his fortress I will take refuge,
    in my God, the most high.

1 From plague and from snare
      you are protected;
you need not fear the dark of night,
and with his wing you will be covered,
delivered from the wicked's might.
    I will dwell . . .

2 There shall no evil overcome you,
neither shall the plague come near;
for he shall place his angels over you
to keep you safe from all your fear.
    I will dwell . . .

3 When I call to the Lord he will answer,
he will set my soul on high;
he will be near in time of trouble,
give long life, and satisfy.
    I will dwell . . .

91C
From Psalm 91, Elaine Davis
© 1985 Ears and Eyes Music Ltd/
Boosey & Hawkes Music Publishers Ltd

1 I will live within the shadow
of the almighty God of all;
by his wings I shall be protected,
for ever trusting in him.
    He alone is my refuge,
    he alone is my God;
    and he'll never, never fail me –
    he is faithful unto me,
    he is faithful unto me.

2 I shall not fear the darkness of night,
   or the dangers of day;
   disaster or fear
        shall never overwhelm me
   while I am trusting in him.
        He alone is my refuge . . .

92A From Psalm 92
         © Christopher Idle/Jubilate Hymns

1 Make music to the Lord most high
   whose praise is our delight:
   we sing your love as day begins,
   your faithfulness by night.

2 Lord, when we see all you have done
   our songs of joy resound:
   your handiwork, how vast it is,
   your counsels, how profound!

WOMEN
3 The godless mind will never know –
   because its sense is void –
   that though the wicked spread like grass,
   they all shall be destroyed.

ALL
4 For ever, Lord, you are supreme;
   your throne remains on high
   while rebels meet eternal doom
   and evil-doers die.

MEN
5 But like the cedar and the palm
   the righteous stand serene;
   they flourish in the house of God,
   their leaves are fresh and green.

ALL
6 To fruitful age they still proclaim
   the Lord who makes them new –
   our God, in whom no wrong is found,
   my Rock, for ever true.

92B From Psalm 92, Tom Howard and Bill Batstone
         © 1982 Maranatha! Music/Word Music (UK)

   It is good to give thanks to the Lord,
   singing praises to our God on high:
   sing of mercies throughout the day
   and of faithfulness by night,
   and of faithfulness by night.

1 I will rejoice in the work of your hands,
   for you have made me glad;
   your enemies scatter, they fall away,
   but the righteous one shall stand!
        It is good to give thanks . . .

2 From the strings of an instrument
   my offering will pour:
   the God of righteousness is my Rock,
   exalted evermore!
        It is good to give thanks . . .

92C From Psalm 92, Good News Bible version
         © American Bible Society

GROUP/CHOIR/SOLO
   How good it is to give thanks to you,
   O Lord;
   to sing in your honour,
   O most high God!

ALL
   How good it is to give thanks to you,
   O Lord;
   to sing in your honour,
   O most high God:

GROUP/CHOIR/SOLO
1 To proclaim your constant love
        every morning
   and your faithfulness every night,
   with the music of stringed instruments
   and with melody on the harp.
   ALL How good it is . . .

GROUP/CHOIR/SOLO
2 Your mighty deeds, O Lord,
        make me glad;
   because of what you have done,
        I sing for joy.
   How great are your actions, Lord;
   how deep are your thoughts!
   ALL How good it is . . .

GROUP/CHOIR/SOLO
3 The righteous will flourish
        like palm trees,
   they will grow
        like the cedars of Lebanon;
   they are like trees planted
        in the house of the Lord,
   that flourish in the Temple of our God.
   ALL How good it is . . .

93A From Psalm 93
         © Michael Saward/Jubilate Hymns

1 Clothed in kingly majesty,
   robed in regal power,
        God is over all.

2 Lord of all, unshakeable,
   throned beyond all time,
        God is over all.

3 Greater than the river's roar
   and the surging sea,
        God is over all.

4   Changeless as his law's decrees,
    crowned our holy king,
        God is over all.

93B
From Psalm 93
© Timothy Dudley-Smith

1   God is King! The Lord is reigning,
        might and majesty his robe;
    to his seat on high ascended,
    girded round with glory splendid,
    there in time and space sustaining
        this our star-encircled globe.
    Foreordained and founded fast,
    evermore his throne shall last!

2   God is King! In storm and thunder
        wind and tide their warfare wage;
    bursting seas and breakers towering,
    pounding surge the rocks devouring,
    lightning rending skies asunder,
        ocean's roar and tempest's rage.
    Mightier far than sea or sky
    stands the throne of God on high!

3   God is King! Let earth adore him –
        changeless still his sure decree.
    Throned beyond our mortal telling,
    holiness and truth his dwelling:
    come with trembling hearts before him,
        bow the head and bend the knee,
    where the ransomed ever raise
    God's imperishable praise!

93L
Psalm 93.1–5
© Editor/Jubilate Hymns

    The Lord reigns, robed in majesty:
A   **he arms himself with power.**

    The earth is firmly set in place:
B   **it never can be moved.**

    Your throne was founded long ago:
A   **before all time began.**

    The oceans raise their voice, O Lord:
B   **and lift their roaring waves.**

    The Lord is mightier than the sea:
A   **he rules supreme on high.**

    His laws stand firm through endless days:
B   **his praise for evermore.**
ALL **Amen.**

    Glory to the Father, and to the Son,
    and to the Holy Spirit:
    as it was in the beginning, is now,
    and shall be for ever. Amen.

The congregation may divide at A *and* B.

95A
From Psalm 95, *Venite*
© Christopher Idle/Jubilate Hymns

1   Come with all joy to sing to God
    our saving rock, the living Lord;
    in glad thanksgiving seek his face
    with songs of victory and grace.

2   In holiness and light arrayed
    above all gods that we have made
    he is the one almighty king
    and his the glory that we sing.

WOMEN
3   The earth is his from east to west,
    from ocean-floor to mountain-crest;
    he made the seas and formed the lands,
    he shaped the islands by his hands.

MEN
4   Come near to worship! come with faith,
    bow down to him who gives us breath:
    God is our shepherd, he alone;
    we are his people, all his own.

WOMEN
5   But if you hear God's voice today
    do not reject what he will say:
    when Israel wandered from God's path
    they suffered forty years of wrath.

MEN
6   That generation went astray,
    they did not want to know his way;
    they put their saviour to the test,
    and saw his power, but lost their rest.

ALL
7   So to the God of earth and heaven,
    the Father, Spirit, Son, be given
    praise now, as praise has ever been
    and ever shall be praise. Amen.

95B
From Psalm 95, *Venite*
© Michael Perry/Jubilate Hymns

1   Come, worship God
        who is worthy of honour,
    enter his presence
        with thanks and a song!
    He is the rock of his people's salvation,
    to whom our jubilant praises belong.

2   Ruled by his might
        are the heights of the mountains,
    held in his hands
        are the depths of the earth;
    his is the sea, his the land,
        for he made them,
    king above all gods,
        who gave us our birth.

3 We are his people,
      the sheep of his pasture,
he is our maker and to him we pray;
gladly we kneel
      in obedience before him –
great is the God
      whom we worship this day!

4 Now let us listen,
      for God speaks among us,
open our hearts
      and receive what he says:
peace be to all
      who remember his goodness,
trust in his word and rejoice in his ways!

95c

Psalm 95, © David Frost
Pointing © Wm Collins

1 O come let us sing ' out · to the ' Lord:
**let us shout in triumph
to the ' rock of ' our sal'vation.**

2 Let us come before his ' face with '
thanksgiving:
**and cry ' out to · him ' joyfully ·
in ' psalms.**

3 For the Lord is a ' great ' God:
and a great ' king a·bove ' all ' gods.

4 In his hand are the ' depths · of the '
earth:
**and the peaks of the ' mountains ·
are ' his ' also.**

Second part

5 The sea is his and ' he ' made it:
his hands ' moulded ' dry ' land.

6 Come let us worship and ' bow ' down:
**and kneel be'fore the ' Lord
our ' maker.**

7 For he is the ' Lord our ' God:
**we are his ' people ·
and the ' sheep of · his ' pasture.**

8 Today if only you would hear his voice *
'Do not harden your ' hearts · as at '
Meribah:
**as on that day at ' Massah '
in the ' wilderness;**

9 when your ' fathers ' tested me:
**put me to proof
though ' they had ' seen my ' works.**

10 'Forty years long I loathed that
gener'ation · and ' said:
**"It is a people who err in their hearts *
for they ' do not ' know my ' ways";**

11 of whom I ' swore · in my ' wrath:
"They ' shall not ' enter · my ' rest."'

Glory to the Father and ' to the ' Son:
and ' to the ' Holy ' Spirit;
as it was in the be'ginning · is ' now:
and shall be for ' ever. ' A'men.

95D

From Psalm 95, *Venite*
© Stephen Dean

ALL
Come, let us sing out with joy
      to the Lord;
hail the rock of salvation!
Come into his presence
      to give him thanks,
singing psalms of triumph.

LEADER/GROUP
1 In his hands are the depths of the earth,
the mountain peaks belong to him;
his is the sea, he created it,
his is the dry land, formed by his hands.
ALL Come, let us sing out . . .

LEADER/GROUP
2 Bow down before him in prayer,
kneel before the Lord and adore:
he is the Lord our shepherd,
we his people, the flock that he feeds.
ALL Come, let us sing out . . .

LEADER/GROUP
3 Listen to the voice of the Lord,
do not grow stubborn
      nor harden your hearts;
put not your God to the test,
well you know how he cares for us.
ALL Come, let us sing out . . .

LEADER/GROUP
4 Praise the Father who made all things,
praise the Son who died for us,
praise the Spirit
      who gladdens our hearts;
praise unceasing fill heaven and earth!
ALL Come, let us sing out . . .

95E

From Psalm 95, *Venite*
© Richard Bewes/Jubilate Hymns

1 Let us sing to the God of salvation,
let us sing to the Lord our rock;
let us come to his house
      with thanksgiving,
let us come before the Lord and sing!
Praise our maker,
praise our saviour,
praise the Lord
our everlasting king:
every throne
must bow before him –
God is Lord of everything!

2 In his hand are the earth's
         deepest places,
  and the strength of the hills is his;
  all the sea is the Lord's, for he made it –
  by his hand the solid rock was formed.
      Praise our maker,
      praise our saviour,
      praise the Lord
      our everlasting king:
      every throne
      must bow before him –
      God is Lord of everything!

3 Let us worship the Lord our maker,
  let us kneel to the Lord our God;
  for we all are the sheep of his pasture –
  he will guide us by his powerful hand.
      Praise our maker . . .

4 Let today be the time when you hear him!
  May our hearts not be hard or cold,
  lest we stray from the Lord in rebellion
  as his people did in time of old.
      Praise our maker . . .

95F

From Psalm 95, *Venite*
© Michael Perry/Jubilate Hymns

1 Come, sing praises to the Lord above,
  rock of our salvation, God of love;
  with delight into his presence move,
  for the Lord our God is king!
      He's the king above the mountains high,
      the sea is his, the land and sky;
      mighty continents and islands lie
      within the hollow of his hand.

2 Come to worship him and bow the knee,
  for the shepherd of the flock is he;
  humble creatures in his hand are we –
  sing the praise of God the king!
      He's the king . . .

3 Hear the story of his people now,
  you with stubborn hearts
         who will not bow;
  learn what happened long ago and how
  God can show you he is king!
      He's the king . . .

4 Forty years he kept the prize away,
  made them wander
         till they walked his way,
  exiled all of them until the day
  they should honour him as king:
      He's the king . . .

95G

From Psalm 95, *Venite*
© Timothy Dudley-Smith

1 Come, let us praise the Lord,
  with joy our God acclaim,
  his greatness tell abroad
  and bless his saving name.
      Lift high your songs
      before his throne
      to whom alone
      all praise belongs.

2 Our God of matchless worth,
  our King beyond compare,
  the deepest bounds of earth,
  the hills, are in his care.
      He all decrees,
      who by his hand
      prepared the land
      and formed the seas.

3 In worship bow the knee,
  our glorious God confess;
  the great Creator, he,
  the Lord our Righteousness.
      He reigns unseen:
      his flock he feeds
      and gently leads
      in pastures green.

4 Come, hear his voice today,
  receive what love imparts;
  his holy will obey
  and harden not your hearts.
      His ways are best;
      and lead at last,
      all troubles past,
      to perfect rest.

95H

From Psalm 95, *Venite*, Brent Chambers
© 1985 Scripture in Song/Thankyou Music

  Come, let us sing for joy to the Lord,
  come, let us sing for joy to the Lord,
  come, let us sing for joy to the Lord,
  come, let us sing for joy to the Lord!

      Come, let us sing for joy to the Lord,
      let us shout aloud
      to the Rock of our salvation;
      come, let us sing . . .

1 Let us come before him
         with thanksgiving,
  and extol him with music and song:
  for the Lord, our Lord, is the great God,
  the great king above all gods.
      Come, let us sing for joy to the Lord,
      let us shout aloud . . .

2 Let us bow before him in our worship,
let us kneel before God, our great king;
for he is our God,
    and we are his people –
that's why we shout and sing:
  Come, let us sing for joy to the Lord,
  let us shout aloud . . .

M&N You shall know his power today –
N if you listen to his voice.

> **Glory to the Father, and to the Son,**
> **and to the Holy Spirit:**
> **as it was in the beginning, is now,**
> **and shall be for ever. Amen.**

The congregation may divide at A and B, the
ministers at M and N.

95I
From Psalm 95, *Venite*
© Paul Inwood/Magnificat Music

Joy, joy, ring out your joy
to the Lord, the saving Lord;
sing, sing, praise him and sing
of his love in all his works!

1 A mighty God is the Lord,
a great King, who holds the earth
in his hands; to him belong
all the seas and mountains,
the heights and the depths of the world.
  Joy, joy, ring . . .

2 Come, let us worship the Lord,
the God who made us;
let us bow down in his sight,
for we are his people,
the sheep of his flock,
and he is our shepherd and pastor.
  Joy, joy, ring . . .

3 Listen today to the voice of the Lord,
and open your hearts to his word;
let your minds
    be not like a barren desert,
but fertile, and watered by faith.
  Joy, joy, ring . . .

95L
Psalm 95.1–7
© Editor/Jubilate Hymns

M Come, let's joyfully praise our God,
acclaiming the Rock of our salvation.

N Come before him with thanksgiving, and
greet him with melody.

A **Our God is a great God –**
B **a king above all other gods.**

A **The depths of the earth are in his**
hands –
B **the mountain peaks belong to him.**

A **The sea is his – he made it!**
B **His own hands prepared the land.**

M Come, bow down to worship him;
N kneel before the Lord who made us.

A&B **We are his people,**
the sheep of his flock.

96A
From Psalm 96
© Stephen Horsfall/Jubilate Hymns

1 Sing a new song
    of glory and salvation,
through all the earth
    let voices now be raised;
speak of God's mighty power
    in every nation –
great is the Lord,
    and greatly to be praised!

2 Sing and adore,
    shout loud with jubilation,
tell of the truth and splendour
    of that Name;
come with thanksgiving,
    worship, all creation –
praise be to God
    for evermore the same.

3 Say to the earth:
    God's rule is never-ending,
soon Christ shall come
    to judge our human race –
anthems of joy
    from earth and heaven blending
as all creation joins
    to sing God's grace!

96B
Psalm 96, © David Frost

CHOIR
O sing to the Lord a new song:
sing to the Lord all the earth.
ALL
O sing to the Lord a new song:
sing to the Lord all the earth.

CHOIR
1 Sing to the Lord and bless his holy name:
proclaim the good news of his salvation
    from day to day.
Declare his glory among the nations:
and his wonders among all peoples.
ALL
O sing to the Lord a new song:
sing to the Lord all the earth.

CHOIR

2 As for all the gods of the nations
        they are mere idols:
it is the Lord who made the heavens.
Majesty and glory are before him:
beauty and power are in his sanctuary.

ALL

    O sing to the Lord a new song:
    sing to the Lord all the earth.

CHOIR

3 O worship the Lord
        in the beauty of his holiness:
let the whole earth stand in awe of him.
Say among the nations
        that the Lord is king:
he shall judge the world
        with righteousness
    and the peoples with his truth.

ALL

    O sing to the Lord a new song:
    sing to the Lord all the earth.
    O sing to the Lord a new song:
    sing to the Lord all the earth.

CHOIR

    O sing a new song!

96C
From Psalm 96, Mick Ray
© 1977 Thankyou Music

    Sing out to the Lord a new song,
    sing out to the Lord, all the earth;
    sing to the Lord, bless his name –
    he is greatly to be praised!
    Sing out to the Lord a new song!

1 Tell among the nations: the Lord reigns,
the world shall never be moved.
Let the heavens be glad
and the earth rejoice!
Sing out to the Lord a new song!
    Sing out to the Lord . . .

2 Then shall all the trees sing for joy
before the Lord – for he comes;
he will judge the world
with his righteousness.
Sing out to the Lord a new song!
    Sing out to the Lord . . .

    Sing out to the Lord a new song!

96D
From Psalm 96, Herbert Chappell
© 1974 Chappell Music Ltd

1 LEADER O sing out to the Lord a new song,
    ALL O sing out to the Lord a new song!
LEADER Bless his name,
    ALL bless his name;
LEADER sing of his glory from day to day.

2 LEADER Declare his wonders
        to all the world,
    ALL declare his wonders
        to all the world.
LEADER Bless his name,
    ALL bless his name:
LEADER honour and majesty
        are in his place.

3 LEADER O worship the Lord
        in the beauty of holiness,
    let the heavens and the sea
        and the fields
    and the trees of the wood rejoice.

4 LEADER O sing out to the Lord a new song,
    ALL O sing out to the Lord a new song!
LEADER Bless his name,
    ALL bless his name:
LEADER for he will come
        to judge the people with his truth.

96E
From Psalm 96
© Michael Perry/Jubilate Hymns

1 Sing to the Lord
    with a song of profound delight,
serve him by day
and bring praises in the night:
    MEN tell of the battles fought for us,
    A marvellous,
    B glorious;
    WOMEN tell of his wonders done for us,
    ALL worthy of acclaim.

2 Beauty and power
are the marks of our Saviour's grace,
splendour and light
shine in glory from his face:
    MEN worship the Lord in holiness,
    A faithfulness,
    B godliness –
    WOMEN judging the world
        with righteousness
    ALL he will come to reign.

3 So let the skies sing aloud
and the earth rejoice –
beasts of the field
and the forest lift their voice:
    MEN firmly he set the solid ground,
    A seas abound,
    B skies resound;
    WOMEN all we desire in God is found –
    ALL glory to his name!

The singers may divide at A *and* B.

96L
Psalm 96.1–13
© Editor/Jubilate Hymns

Sing to the Lord a new song:
A **sing to the Lord, all the earth.**

Sing to the Lord, praise his name:
B **proclaim his salvation each day.**

Declare his glory among the nations:
A **his marvellous deeds
among the peoples.**

Great is the Lord, and worthy of praise:
B **honour him above all gods.**

Splendour and majesty surround him:
A **power and beauty fill his temple.**

Praise the Lord, all people on earth:
B **praise his glory and might.**

Give him the glory due to his name:
A **bring an offering into his temple.**

Worship the Lord in his beauty and
holiness:
B **tremble before him, all the earth.**

Say to the nations:
ALL **The Lord is king!**

Let the heavens rejoice and the earth be
glad:
A **let all creation sing for joy.**

For God shall come to judge the world:
B **and rule the people with his truth.
Amen.**

The congregation may divide at A and B.

97
From Psalm 97
© Timothy Dudley-Smith

1 The everlasting Lord is king –
   let ocean find a voice,
   her furthest shores his triumph sing
   and all the earth rejoice.

2 He comes in clouds with fire and flame
   to make his judgements known;
   the mountains tremble at his name
   and melt before his throne.

3 The sun and moon and starry sky
   his glories blaze abroad,
   the one eternal God most high,
   the true and living Lord.

4 Defended by his hand divine
   his saints secure remain;
   for them the light of life shall shine,
   the King of love shall reign.

97L
Psalm 97.1–12
© Editor/Jubilate Hymns

The Lord is king:
the Lord is king!

Let the whole wide earth rejoice:
A **let the islands all be glad.**

Thunder-clouds encircle him:
B **truth and justice are his throne.**

Fire shall go before the Lord:
C **burning up his enemies.**

Lightning strikes the darkened world:
A **all the people see and fear.**

Mountains melt before our God:
B **he is Lord of all the earth.**

Skies proclaim his righteousness:
C **nations see his glory now.**

Idol-worshippers are shamed:
A **gods bow down before the Lord.**

Let Jerusalem rejoice:
B **in your faithful judgements, Lord!**

Sovereign of the universe:
C **mightier still than all the gods!**

Yet you help your saints, O Lord:
A **saving them from wicked men.**

Light will shine upon the good:
B **gladness fill the righteous heart.**

Now recall what God has done:
C **thank him,**
B **praise him,**
ALL **and rejoice!**

**Glory to the Father, and to the Son,
and to the Holy Spirit:
as it was in the beginning, is now,
and shall be for ever. Amen.**

The congregation may divide at A, B and C.

98A
From Psalm 98, *Cantate Domino*
© Michael Baughen/Jubilate Hymns

1 Sing to God new songs of worship –
   all his deeds are marvellous;
   he has brought salvation to us
   with his hand and holy arm.
   He has shown to all the nations
   righteousness and saving power;
   he recalled his truth and mercy
   to his people Israel.

2 Sing to God new songs of worship –
earth has seen his victory;
let the lands of earth be joyful
praising him with thankfulness.
Sound upon the harp his praises,
play to him with melody;
let the trumpets sound his triumph,
show your joy to God the king!

3 Sing to God new songs of worship –
let the sea now make a noise;
all on earth and in the waters,
sound your praises to the Lord.
Let the hills rejoice together,
let the rivers clap their hands,
for with righteousness and justice
he will come to judge the earth.

98B
From Psalm 98, *Cantate Domino*
© Timothy Dudley-Smith

1 Sing a new song to the Lord,
he to whom wonders belong!
Rejoice in his triumph
        and tell of his power –
O sing to the Lord a new song!

2 Now to the ends of the earth
see his salvation is shown:
and still he remembers
        his mercy and truth,
unchanging in love to his own.

3 Sing a new song and rejoice,
publish his praises abroad!
Let voices in chorus
        with trumpet and horn,
resound for the joy of the Lord!

4 Join with the hills and the sea
thunders of praise to prolong!
In judgement and justice
        he comes to the earth –
O sing to the Lord a new song!

98C
Psalm 98, *Cantate Domino*
© David Frost, Pointing © Wm Collins

1 O sing to the Lord a ' new ' song:
for he has ' done ' marvel·lous ' things;
2 his right hand and his ' holy ' arm:
they have ' got ' him the ' victory.

3 The Lord has made ' known · his
sal'vation:
**he has revealed his just de'liverance ·
in the ' sight of · the ' nations.**
4 He has remembered his mercy and
faithfulness towards the ' house of ' Israel:
**and all the ends of the earth
have seen the sal'vation ' of our ' God.**

5 Shout with joy to the Lord ' all the ' earth:
**break into ' singing ·
and ' make ' melody.**
6 Make melody to the Lord up'on the '
harp:
**upon the harp
and ' with the ' sounds of ' praise.**

7 With trumpets ' and with ' horns:
**cry out in triumph
be'fore the ' Lord the ' king.**
8 Let the sea roar and ' all that ' fills it:
**the good earth
and ' those who ' live up'on it.**

9 Let the rivers ' clap their ' hands:
**and let the mountains
ring out to'gether · be'fore the ' Lord;**
10 for he comes to ' judge the ' earth:
**he shall judge the world
  with righteousness *
and the ' peoples ' with ' equity.**

**Glory to the Father and ' to the ' Son:
and ' to the ' Holy ' Spirit;
as it was in the be'ginning · is ' now:
and shall be for ' ever. ' A'men.**

98D
From Psalm 98, *Cantate Domino*
© Michael Perry/Jubilate Hymns

1 Lift up your hearts to the Lord,
break into songs of joy;
let the sea roar, let the hills ring,
shout his glorious name!
    Harps and horns and trumpets, sound;
    praise him, all the world around!
    O sing a new song;
    O sing a new song!

2 Bow down and worship the Lord,
greet him who comes to reign;
share his triumph, hear his judgement,
see his marvellous works:
    Harps and horns . . .

3 Tell out the word of the Lord,
speak of his saving power:
sure his mercy, true his promise,
great his wonderful love!
    Harps and horns . . .

98L
Psalm 98.1–9
© Editor/Jubilate Hymns

Sing to the Lord a new song:
for he has done marvellous things.

His right hand and his holy arm:
have brought a great triumph to us.

A **He lets his salvation be known:**
B **his righteousness seen by the world.**
A **To us he continues his love:**
B **his glory is witnessed by all.**

Shout for joy to the Lord, all the earth:
ALL **and burst into jubilant song.**

A **Make music to God with the harp:**
B **with songs**
   and the sound of your praise.
A **With trumpets and blast of the horn:**
B **sing praises to God as your king.**

Let rivers and streams clap their hands:
ALL **the mountains together sing praise.**

The Lord comes to judge the whole
earth:
in righteousness God rules the world.
Amen.

The congregation may divide at A and B.

99A
From Psalm 99
© Michael Saward/Jubilate Hymns

1 God is king – the nations tremble,
he is throned – the earth is quaking;
Lord supreme, the people praise him:
   Holy, holy, holy!

2 God is king – he calls for justice,
he proclaims his righteous judgement;
Lord supreme, the people praise him:
   Holy, holy, holy!

3 God is king, yet all may know him –
priests and prophets heard his precepts;
Lord supreme, the people praise him:
   Holy, holy, holy!

4 God is king, yet he forgives us,
bears our sins in his own body;
Lord supreme, the people praise him:
   Holy, holy, holy!

99B
From Psalm 99, Phil Rogers
© 1985 Thankyou Music

The Lord reigns:
let the nations tremble –
he sits enthroned
between the cherubim –
let the earth shake!
The Lord reigns . . .

Great is the Lord in Zion,
exalted above all the nations:
let them praise
   his great and awesome name.
The Lord reigns . . .

Holy is he,
holy is he,
holy is the Lord.

Mighty is he . . .

Gracious is he . . .

Worthy is he . . .

99L
Psalm 99.1–9
© Editor/Jubilate Hymns

The Lord reigns:
A **let the nations tremble!**

He sits enthroned on high:
B **let the earth shake!**

Great is the Lord our God:
ALL **exalted over all the world.**

Let the nations praise his awesome name,
and say:
A **God is holy!**

Praise the Lord our God, and worship at
his feet:
B **God is holy!**

Exalt the Lord our God, and worship on
his holy mountain:
ALL **The Lord our God is holy!**

Glory to the Father, and to the Son,
and to the Holy Spirit:
as it was in the beginning, is now,
and shall be for ever. Amen.

The congregation may divide at A and B.

100A
From Psalm 100, *Jubilate Deo*
© Michael Baughen/Jubilate Hymns

1 Come, rejoice before your maker
all you peoples of the earth;
serve the Lord your God with gladness,
come before him with a song!

2 Know for certain that Jehovah
is the true and only God:
we are his, for he has made us;
we are sheep within his fold.

3 Come with grateful hearts before him,
enter now his courts with praise;
show your thankfulness towards him,
give due honour to his name.

4 For the Lord our God is gracious –
everlasting in his love;
and to every generation
his great faithfulness endures.

100B
From Psalm 100, *Jubilate Deo*
© James Quinn SJ/Geoffrey Chapman

1 Sing, all creation, sing to God in gladness,
   joyously serve him,
         singing hymns of homage;
   chanting his praises,
         come before his presence:
      praise the Almighty!

2 Know that our God is Lord of all the ages;
   he is our maker: we are all his creatures,
   people he fashioned,
         sheep he leads to pasture:
      praise the Almighty!

3 Enter his temple, ringing out his praises;
   sing in thanksgiving
         as you come before him;
   blessing his bounty, glorify his greatness:
      praise the Almighty!

4 Great in his goodness
         is the Lord we worship;
   steadfast his kindness,
         love that knows no ending;
   faithful his word is,
         changeless, everlasting:
      praise the Almighty!

100C
Psalm 100, *Jubilate Deo*
© David Frost, Pointing © Wm Collins

1 O shout to the Lord in triumph | all the |
   earth:
   serve the Lord with gladness *
   and come before his | face
      with | songs of | joy.
2 Know that the Lord | he is | God:
   it is he who has made us
   and we are his; *
   we are his | people ·
   and the | sheep of · his | pasture.

3 Come into his gates with thanksgiving *
   and into his | courts with | praise:
   give thanks to him
   and | bless his | holy | name.
4 For the Lord is good *
   his loving mercy | is for | ever:
   his faithfulness
   through|out all | gener|ations.

   Glory to the Father and | to the | Son:
   and | to the | Holy | Spirit;
   as it was in the be|ginning is | now:
   and shall be for | ever. | A|men.

100D
From Psalm 100, *Jubilate Deo*
© David Preston/Jubilate Hymns

1 With joyful shouts acclaim the Lord,
   all people everywhere;
   bow down to him in glad accord,
   with songs of joy draw near!

2 Acknowledge God the Lord to be
   the one true God indeed:
   he made us all, his sheep are we,
   that in his pastures feed.

3 As you approach his temple steps
   your thankfulness proclaim;
   come in with praises on your lips
   and bless his holy name.

4 Rejoice because the Lord is good,
   his steadfast love is sure;
   his faithfulness has always stood
   and shall for evermore.

100E
From Psalm 100, *Jubilate Deo*
Author unknown

   I will enter his gates with thanksgiving
         in my heart,
   I will enter his courts with praise:
   I will say this is the day
         that the Lord has made,
   I will rejoice for he has made me glad.

   He has made me glad,
         he has made me glad,
   I will rejoice for he has made me glad.
   He has made me glad,
         he has made me glad,
   I will rejoice for he has made me glad.

100F
From Psalm 100, *Jubilate Deo*
© David Frost

   A O shout to the Lord in triumph
         all the earth,
   B O shout to the Lord in triumph
         all the earth;
   A Serve the Lord with gladness,
   B serve the Lord with gladness,
   A and come before his face
         with songs of joy,
   A and come before his face
         with songs of joy!

   A O shout to the Lord . . .

1 ALL Know that the Lord, he is God;
         it is he who has made us
            and we are his:
         we are his people
         and the sheep of his pasture.

A Come into his gates
    with thanksgiving,
B come into his gates
    with thanksgiving,
A and into his courts with praise,
B and into his courts with praise;
A give thanks to him
    and bless his holy name,
B give thanks to him
    and bless his holy name.

2 ALL For the Lord, the Lord is good:
    his loving mercy is for ever,
    his faithfulness
    throughout all generations.

A O shout to the Lord . . .

A Come into his gates . . .

100G

From Psalm 100, *Jubilate Deo*
After Michael Perry
Fred Dunn © 1977, 1980 Thankyou Music

Jubilate, everybody,
serve the Lord in all your ways,
and come before his presence singing;
enter now his courts with praise.
For the Lord our God is gracious,
and his mercy's everlasting,
Jubilate, jubilate, jubilate Deo.

100H

From Psalm 100, *Jubilate Deo*

Come, rejoice before him;
sing to God your praises:
    Alleluia!

Come, rejoice . . .

OR:
*Jubilate Deo,
jubilate Deo,
    Alleluia!*

Jubilate . . .

100I

From Psalm 100, *Jubilate Deo*
Jacques Berthier
© 1978, 1980, 1981 Taizé/Wm Collins

Come, rejoice in God;
praise him, all the earth.
Serve your God, serve your God,
gladly serve your God!

Alleluia, alleluia,
gladly serve your God;
alleluia, alleluia,
gladly serve your God!

*Jubilate Deo omnis terra,
servite Domino in laetitia,
alleluia, alleluia, in laetitia!
Alleluia, alleluia, in laetitia!*

100J

From Psalm 100, *Jubilate Deo*
© Stephen Wilcockson

1 O be glad in the Lord, and rejoice –
    all you lands of the earth, come and sing;
    with his praises now lift up your voice,
    to his presence your thanksgiving bring!
    Our creator is God, be assured –
    it is not by ourselves we were made;
    God himself is our Shepherd and Lord,
    in his hand we shall not be afraid!

2 Through his gates let us gratefully move;
    to his courts let us come with our praise!
    O give thanks to the Lord for his love;
    O rejoice in his works and his ways!
    For our God is abounding in grace,
    and his mercy is faithful and sure:
    generations to come, seek his face,
    praise and worship the Lord evermore!

100K

From Psalm 100, *Jubilate Deo*
John Daniels
© 1986 Word Music (UK)

1 Shout for joy and sing,
    serve the Lord your king,
    coming before him
    joyfully – and sing,
    knowing that the Lord is God;
    he has made us, we are his –
    in his pasture we have food
    and in his presence live (evermore).

Shout for joy . . .

2 Enter in his gates
    and his courts with praise,
    giving thanks to him
    throughout all our days:
    for the Lord our God is good,
    and his love has ever stood;
    faithfully he keeps his word
    and his love to all (generations).

Enter in his gates . . .

100L

Psalm 100.1–5
© Editor/Jubilate Hymns

Rejoice in the Lord, all the earth:
worship the Lord with gladness.

Remember the Lord is our God:
A **we are his flock and he made us.**

Come to his temple with praise:
B **enter his gates with thanksgiving.**

The love of the Lord will not fail:
God will be faithful for ever. Amen.

The congregation may divide at A *and* B.

100M

From Psalm 100, *Jubilate Deo*
Tom Brooks
© 1985 Integrity's Hosanna! Music

Shout! Shout joyfully to your God,
    all the earth!
Shout! Shout joyfully to your God,
    all the earth!
Sing the glory of his name
and make his praises glorious.
Shout! Shout joyfully to your God,
    all the earth!

Shout! . . .

    Joyfully, joyfully,
    all the earth shall bow the knee;
    joyfully, joyfully,
    we will sing in harmony,
    singing praises to your name!

Shout . . .

100N

From Psalm 100, *Jubilate Deo*
Jonathan Asprey
© 1975 Celebration/Thankyou Music

    O be joyful in the Lord,
    O be joyful in the Lord,
    let us make a joyful noise,
    let the whole earth rejoice;
    O be joyful in the Lord,
    all you lands!

1 Know that the Lord he is God:
  he has made us we are his;
  we are the sheep of his pasture,
  the people of his hand.
    O be joyful . . .

2 Enter his gates with thanksgiving,
  come into his courts with praise;
  be thankful now to him,
  and speak good of his name.
    O be joyful . . .

3 Know that the Lord he is good:
  his love lasts for ever;
  he's faithful and true
  through every generation.
    O be joyful . . .

101

From Psalm 101
© David Mowbray/Jubilate Hymns

1 With heart and hands washed clean
  I'll sing your praise, O Lord –
  a song of mercy, yet a song
  of judgement and the sword:

2 For wickedness must pass
  like smoke, and drift away;
  deceit and pride shall be cast down
  like idols made of clay.

3 Walk with me in God's house,
  all of you of upright heart:
  for those who keep his company
  no force can tear apart.

102A

From Psalm 102
© Michael Perry/Jubilate Hymns

1 You laid the foundations of earth,
  the heavens
      were wrought by your hands;
  they perish, but you will remain,
  they falter, but your glory stands.

2 Like clothing
      the worlds shall be changed,
  the skies cast away like a veil;
  but you, Lord, are always the same,
  your years like your words never fail.

3 Your servants shall trust in your love,
  our children shall walk in your ways,
  till time holds us captive no more
  and paradise rings with your praise!

102B

From Psalm 102
© Christopher Hayward/Jubilate Hymns

    Hear my prayer, O Lord,
    hear my prayer, O Lord;
    let my cry for help
    come to you.

    Do not hide your face from me
    when I am in distress;
    turn your ear to me.
    When I call,
    answer me quickly,
    answer me quickly;
    turn your ear to me.
      Hear my prayer . . .

103A

From Psalm 103
© Timothy Dudley-Smith

1 Praise the Lord and bless his name,
life and peace in him are found.
All his benefits proclaim,
grace with love and mercy crowned:
  sins forgiven, strength restored!
  Sing my soul, and praise the Lord!

2 High as heaven's furthest star,
vaster than the shores of space,
so he bears our sins afar,
so he brings to us his grace.
  He who hears his children's prayer
  ever keeps us in his care.

3 Swifter than the winds that pass,
fading as the summer flowers,
what though all our days are grass?
faith and hope shall still be ours.
  God's unchanging love is sure
  and endures for evermore.

4 Praise the Lord of earth and heaven,
angel hosts about his throne,
sinners by his grace forgiven,
saints who his dominion own:
  God of all, by all adored!
  Sing, my soul, and praise the Lord!

103B

Psalm 103, © David Frost
Pointing © Wm Collins

1 Praise the Lord ˈ O my ˈ soul:
and all that is within me ˈ
  praise his ˈ holy ˈ name.

2 Praise the Lord ˈ O my ˈ soul:
and forˈget not ˈ all his ˈ benefits,

3 who forgives ˈ all your ˈ sin:
and ˈ heals ˈ all · your inˈfirmities,

4 who redeems your ˈ life · from the ˈ Pit:
and crowns you with ˈ mercy ˈ
  and comˈpassion;

Second part

5 who satisfies your being with ˈ good ˈ
things:
so that your ˈ youth · is reˈnewed ·
  like an ˈ eagle's.

6 The Lord ˈ works ˈ righteousness:
and justice
  for ˈ all who ˈ are opˈpressed.

7 He made known his ˈ ways to ˈ Moses:
and his ˈ works ·
  to the ˈ children · of ˈ Israel.

8 The Lord is full of comˈpassion · and ˈ
mercy:
slow to anger ˈ
and of ˈ great ˈ goodness.

9 He will not ˈ always · be ˈ chiding:
nor will he ˈ keep his ˈ anger ·
  for ˈ ever.

10 He has not dealt with us acˈcording · to
our ˈ sins:
nor rewarded us
  acˈcording ˈ to our ˈ wickedness.

11 For as the heavens are high aˈbove the ˈ
earth:
so great is his ˈ mercy ·
  over ˈ those that ˈ fear him;

12 as far as the east is ˈ from the ˈ west:
so far has he ˈ set our ˈ sins ˈ from us.

13 As a father is tender toˈwards his ˈ
children:
so is the Lord ˈ tender ·
  to ˈ those that ˈ fear him.

Second part

14 For he knows of ˈ what · we are ˈ made:
he reˈmembers ·
  that we ˈ are but ˈ dust.

15 The days of man are ˈ but as ˈ grass:
he flourishes ˈ
  like a ˈ flower · of the ˈ field;

16 when the wind goes over it ˈ it is ˈ gone:
and its ˈ place will ˈ know it ·
  no ˈ more.

17 But the merciful goodness of the Lord *
endures for ever and ever toward ˈ
those that ˈ fear him:
and his righteousness
  upˈon their ˈ children's ˈ children;

18 upon those who ˈ keep his ˈ covenant:
and reˈmember ·
  his comˈmandments · to ˈ do them.

19 The Lord has established his ˈ throne in ˈ
heaven:
and his ˈ kingdom ˈ rules · over ˈ all.

20 Praise the Lord all you his angels * you
that exˈcel in ˈ strength:
you that fulfil his word
and obey
  the ˈ voice of ˈ his comˈmandment.

21 Praise the Lord all ˈ you his ˈ hosts:
his ˈ servants · who ˈ do his ˈ will.

22 Praise the Lord all his works *
in all places of ˈ his doˈminion:
praise the ˈ Lord ˈ O my ˈ soul!

Glory to the Father and ⎮ to the ⎮ Son:
and ⎮ to the ⎮ Holy ⎮ Spirit;
as it was in the be⎮ginning · is ⎮ now:
and shall be for ⎮ ever. ⎮ A⎮men.

103C

From Psalm 103, © David Frost

The Lord is full of compassion and mercy:
slow to anger and of great goodness.

He will not always be chiding:
nor will he keep his anger for ever.

He has not dealt with us
        according to our sins:
nor rewarded us
        according to our wickedness.

For as the heavens
        are high above the earth:
so great is his mercy
        over those that fear him;

as far as the east is from the west:
so far has he set our sins from us.

As a father is tender towards his children:
so is the Lord tender
        to those that fear him.

For he knows of what we are made:
he remembers that we are but dust.

The days of man are but as grass:
he flourishes like a flower of the field;

when the wind goes over it it is gone:
and its place will know it no more.

But the merciful goodness of the Lord
endures for ever and ever
        toward those that fear him:
and his righteousness
        upon their children's children;

upon those who keep his covenant:
and remember his commandments to do
        them.

Glory to the Father and to the Son:
and to the Holy Spirit;
as it was in the beginning is now:
and shall be for ever. Amen.

103D

From Psalm 103, Jacques Berthier
© 1982, 1983, 1984 Taizé/Wm Collins

CONTINUOUS RESPONSE — ALL

Bless the Lord, my soul,
and bless his holy name;
bless the Lord, my soul,
he rescues me from death.

SOLO

1   It is he who forgives all your guilt,
    who heals every one of your ills,
    who redeems your life from the grave,
    who crowns you
            with love and compassion.

SOLO

2   The Lord is compassion and love,
    slow to anger, and rich in mercy;
    he does not treat us according to our sins,
    nor repay us according to our faults.

SOLO

3   As a father has compassion
            on his children,
    the Lord has pity on those who fear him;
    for he knows of what we are made,
    he remembers that we are but dust.

103E

From Psalm 103, Author unknown
© copyright controlled

Bless the Lord, O my soul,
bless the Lord, O my soul,
and all that is within me
bless his holy name;
bless the Lord . . .
    King of kings (for ever and ever),
    Lord of lords (for ever and ever),
    King of kings (for ever and ever),
    King of kings and Lord of lords!

Bless the Lord . . .

103F

From Psalm 103, John Bell
© 1988 The Iona Community/
Wild Goose Publications

O bless the Lord (O my soul),
O bless the Lord (O my soul),
O bless the Lord, bless the Lord
and never forget his love;
O bless the Lord (O my soul),
O bless the Lord (O my soul),
O bless the Lord, bless the Lord
and never forget his love!

103G

From Psalm 103
© Michael Baughen/Jubilate Hymns

Bless the Lord, O my soul,
and all within me, honour his name;
bless the Lord, O my soul,
and never forget all his blessings.

1 He forgives all your sin
   and he heals all your ills;
   he redeems your life from the pit,
   he shows mercy upon you
   and steadfast love;
   he renews your youth by good things.
      Bless the Lord . . .

2 Justice for the oppressed
   with compassion and grace,
   slow to anger, abounding in love:
   he is not always chiding
   but in his love
   he does not remember our sins.
      Bless the Lord . . .

3 As the heavens are high,
   so to those who fear God
   his compassion and mercy are great;
   he removes our sins from us
   and all our guilt
   as far as the East from the West.
      Bless the Lord . . .

4 All our days are like grass
   or a flower of the field –
   as the wind passes over, it goes;
   but on those who obey him,
   with steadfast love
   he bestows his love evermore.
      Bless the Lord . . .

   Bless the Lord, king of all,
   all you his angels doing his word;
   bless the Lord, all his hosts,
   and all of his works in creation!
   Bless the Lord, O my soul!

103L

Psalm 103.1–22
© Editor/Jubilate Hymns

Praise the Lord, my soul:
A **all my being, praise his holy name!**

Praise the Lord, my soul:
B **and do not forget how generous he is.**

A **He forgives all my sins:**
B **and heals all my diseases.**
A **He keeps me from the grave:**
B **and blesses me with love and mercy.**

The Lord is gracious and compassionate:
A **slow to become angry,**
B **and full of constant love.**

He does not keep on rebuking:
A **he is not angry for ever.**

He does not punish us as we deserve:
B **or repay us for our wrongs.**

As far as the earth from the west:
A **so far**
   does he remove our sins from us.

As kind as a father to his children:
B **so kind is the Lord to those who**
   honour him.

Praise the Lord, all his creation:
ALL **praise the Lord, my soul! Amen.**

The congregation may divide at A and B.

103H

From Psalm 103, Berj Topalian
© GNU Productions

Bless the Lord, O my soul,
bless his holy name (bless the Lord):
everlasting is his love,
from age to age the same!

1 Forget not all his benefits –
   he pardons all your sin;
   he heals your infirmities,
   redeems you from death's sting.
      Bless the Lord . . .

2 He crowns you with his steadfast love,
   he fills you with good things;
   your vigour daily he renews –
   you rise on eagles' wings!
      Bless the Lord . . .

104A

From Psalm 104, Brian Foley
© 1971 Faber Music Ltd

1 All things I see, Lord, call to me
      to speak their maker's praise:
   how you have brought them all to be
      and guide them in their ways.

2 I see your beauty in the dawn,
      your goodness in the light;
   I see your power in winds and storm,
      your wisdom in the night.

3 Your waters gather in the skies
      and fall to fill the seas;
   your lands,
         the mountains where they rise,
      are ordered as you please.

4 All things that grow, all things that live,
      and I myself make known
   what praise, what glory I must give
      to you, my God, alone.

104B

From Psalm 104
© Michael Perry/Jubilee Hymns

1 'O bless the Lord, my soul!' I sing,
   and worship day and night
   my God arrayed in majesty
   and robed in glorious light:

2 For like a tent you spread the sky,
   on chariot-clouds you ride;
   and by the wind, your messenger,
   your truth is prophesied.

MEN
3 You bind the sea, or loose the storm
   in lightning's primal flame;
   the rising spring and flowing stream
   cry glory to your name.

ALL
4 O mighty Lord of every land,
   you know our human need,
   and all the creatures of the earth
   you guide and tend and feed.

WOMEN
5 The sun and moon appear and set
   controlled by hidden force;
   the stars declare your faithfulness,
   consistent in their course.

ALL
6 Yet what you give, O sovereign Lord,
   your power can take away;
   our life and death belong to you
   until our dying day.

7 So let me sing your worthy praise,
   your matchless grace extol
   till all creation join the hymn:
   'O bless the Lord, my soul!'

104C

From Psalm 104
© Michael Perry/Jubilee Hymns

1 The majesty of mountains,
   the sovereignty of skies,
   the regal rocks that arch above
   where veils of vapour rise,
   are gifts of God, the Lord of love,
   the worshipful, the wise.

2 The running of the river,
   the surging of the sea,
   the grass that grows high on the hill,
   the flower and fruiting tree,
   our Saviour sends us, by whose will
   all creatures came to be.

3 The glory of the Godhead,
   the Spirit and the Son,
   the Father, faithful down the days:
   to them, the Three-in-One,
   while life shall last be perfect praise
   and highest honour done!

104D

From Psalm 104, Peter and Hanneke Jacobs
© 1984 Maranatha! Music/Word Music (UK)

Bless the Lord, O my soul –
O Lord, you are so great!
Bless the Lord, O my soul:
I will be glad in him.

1 You made all things upon the earth,
   the oceans and the land;
   and every creature in this world
   was made by your command.
   Bless the Lord . . .

2 For all your works I'll praise you Lord,
   I will rejoice in you;
   and from my heart I'll sing this song
   so that I might bless you.
   Bless the Lord . . .

   . . . I'll be glad in him.

104E

From Psalm 104, Donya Brockway
© 1972 Birdwing Music/
Cherry Lane Music Ltd

I will sing out to the Lord as long as I live,
I will sing praise to my God
   while I have my being;
my meditation of him shall be sweet,
I will be glad, I will be glad in the Lord.

Bless the Lord, O my soul,
praise the Lord;
bless the Lord, O my soul,
praise the Lord!

Bless the Lord . . .

104F

From Psalm 104
© Paul Whitell

MEN O praise the Lord O my soul,
WOMEN O praise the Lord O my soul,
ALL O praise the Lord O my soul!

1 Lord, to you all glory be,
   honour, power and majesty:
   you rule over land and sea,
   I'll praise you Lord for ever!

MEN O praise the Lord O my soul,
WOMEN O praise the Lord O my soul,
ALL O praise the Lord O my soul!

2 You have made the grass to grow
and the seasons come and go,
the rivers you caused to flow,
I'll praise you Lord for ever!

MEN O praise the Lord O my soul,
WOMEN O praise the Lord O my soul,
ALL O praise the Lord O my soul!

3 All my life I'll sing to you,
and rejoice in all you do,
I'll offer my prayers to you,
I'll praise you Lord for ever!

MEN O praise the Lord O my soul,
WOMEN O praise the Lord O my soul,
ALL O praise the Lord O my soul!

104L
Psalm 104.1–4, 29–30
© Editor/Jubilate Hymns

O Lord our God, you are very great:
**you are clothed
with splendour and majesty.**

You make winds your messengers:
A **and flashes of fire your servants.**

How many are your works:
B **the earth is full of your creatures!**

When you hide your face, they are
afraid:
A **when you take away their breath,
they die.**

When you send your Spirit they are
created:
B **and you renew the face of the earth.**

**Glory to the Father, and to the Son,
and to the Holy Spirit:
as it was in the beginning, is now,
and shall be for ever. Amen.**

The congregation may divide at A *and* B, *in
which case the* Gloria *should be used.*

105A
From Psalm 105, Chris Bowater
© 1982 Lifestyle Ministries/Word Music (UK)

The Lord has led forth his people
with joy,
and his chosen ones
with singing, singing;
the Lord has led forth his people
with joy,
and his chosen ones with singing.

He has given to them
the lands of the nations,
to possess the fruit and keep his laws,
and praise, praise his name.
The Lord has led forth . . .

105B
From Psalm 105, Christine Mitchell-Innes
© 1986 Ears and Eyes Music Ltd/
Boosey & Hawkes Music Publishers Ltd

Let the hearts of those who seek the Lord
rejoice, rejoice;
let the hearts of those who seek the Lord
rejoice, rejoice:
give praise to him, give thanks to him,
tell of his wonderful works –
let the hearts of those who love the Lord
rejoice!

105L
Psalm 105.1–45
© Editor/Jubilate Hymns

Give thanks to the Lord, praise his name:
A **tell the nations what he has done.**

Sing to him, sing praise to him:
B **tell of all his wonderful deeds.**

Glory in his holy name:
C **let all who worship him rejoice.**

Go to the Lord for help:
A **and worship him for ever.**

Remember the wonders he does:
B **the miracles he performs.**

He is the Lord our God:
C **he judges the whole wide earth.**

He keeps his word and covenant:
A **for a thousand generations.**

The covenant he made with Abraham:
B **the oath he swore to Israel.**

He brought them out of Egypt:
C **and none of them was lost.**

He gave a cloud for covering:
A **a pillar of fire by night.**

He gave them bread from heaven:
B **and water from the rock.**

He brought his people out rejoicing:
C **his chosen ones with shouts of joy.**

ALL **Praise the Lord!**

**Glory to the Father, and to the Son,
and to the Holy Spirit:
as it was in the beginning, is now,
and shall be for ever. Amen.**

*The congregation – and ministers/leaders –
may divide at A, B and C.*

106A
From Psalm 106
© Paul Wigmore/Jubilate Hymns

1 Alleluia! Love eternal
flows from God's most gracious heart.
Who can show how great the Lord is?
Where the skill and where the art?
    Alleluia, alleluia!

2 Though his people sinned against him,
worshipped gods of wood and stone,
he delivered, loved and blessed them!
Was such mercy ever shown?
    Alleluia, alleluia!

3 Save us, Lord, in your great goodness,
hear us calling, now as then;
as our praises rise to greet you,
let the people say, 'Amen!'
    Alleluia, alleluia!

106B
From Psalm 106, John Bell
© 1988 The Iona Community/
Wild Goose Publications

SOLO
1 It is good to give thanks to the Lord,
to remember all he has done;
then God will remember our praises
when he looks with love on his people.
    ALL
    O give thanks to the Lord,
    for his love endures for ever;
    O give thanks to the Lord,
    for the Lord alone is good.

SOLO
2 Our sin is the sin of our fathers,
we have done wrong,
    we all have been evil;
like those who once lived in bondage,
we paid no heed to all you had done.
ALL O give thanks . . .

SOLO
3 Our fathers forsook your love,
at the Red Sea,
    they questioned their God;
they fell from their faith in the desert,
and put God to the test in the wilderness.
ALL O give thanks . . .

SOLO
4 Time after time he would rescue them,
yet in malice they dared to defy him;
despite this he came to their aid
when he heard their cries of distress.
ALL O give thanks . . .

SOLO
5 Save us, O Lord, in your love,
bring us back from all that offends you;
look not alone at our sins,
but remember your promise of mercy.
ALL O give thanks . . .

SOLO
6 Blessed be the Lord God of Israel
both now and through all eternity;
let nations and people cry out
and sing, Amen! Alleluia!
ALL O give thanks . . .

107
From Psalm 107
© David Mowbray/Jubilate Hymns

1 'Give God thanks for he is gracious!'
now may Israel truly say;
through great trials he has brought us
to the dawn of this new day.
    All God's children, all God's children
    praise the wonders he has done
        (he has done);
    praise the wonders he has done!

2 When God's people walked the desert,
hungry, thirsty, faint of heart;
he prepared for them a city,
gave them hope and took their part.
    All God's children . . .

3 Those who steer their ships
        through trouble,
ride the storm and plumb the deep,
reach at length their promised haven,
bless that grace which brings them sleep.
    All God's children . . .

4 Give God thanks for all his mercies:
fields are watered, crops are sown,
sheep and cattle fill the pastures,
babes in arms have safely grown.
    All God's children . . .

107L
Psalm 107.1–31
© Editor/Jubilate Hymns

Give thanks to the Lord, for he is good:
his love endures for ever.

Repeat these words in praise to the Lord:
all those he has redeemed.

Some sailed the ocean in ships:
A **they earned their way on the seas.**

They saw what the Lord can do:
B **his wonderful deeds in the deep.**

For he spoke and stirred up a storm:
A **and lifted high the waves.**

Their ships were thrown in the air:
B **and plunged into the depths.**

Their courage melted away:
A **they reeled like drunken men.**

They came to the end of themselves:
B **and cried to the Lord in their trouble.**

He brought them out of distress:
A **and stilled the raging storm.**

They were glad because of the calm:
B **he brought them safely to harbour.**

Let them give thanks to the Lord:
ALL **for his unfailing love.**

**Glory to the Father, and to the Son,
and to the Holy Spirit:
as it was in the beginning, is now,
and shall be for ever. Amen.**

The congregation may divide at A and B.

108A
From Psalm 108
© Christopher Idle/Jubilate Hymns

1 My heart is ready, O my God:
let songs of joy be born,
let music sound from strings and voice –
I will awake the dawn!

2 Across the continents I sing,
and growing praise shall rise;
for your great love
      spans earth and heaven,
your truth surmounts the skies.

WOMEN
3 O God, be praised above the heavens;
let glory fill the earth,
and help and save with your right hand
the race you brought to birth.

MEN
4 God speaks from his pure sanctuary
to claim both west and east:
'The plains and mountains all are mine,
the greatest and the least.'

WOMEN
5 'My people are my battle-dress,
my sceptre, helm, and sword;
while rebel nations have become
a footstool for the Lord!'

MEN
6 Who else can give us victory
and break the strongholds down?
O God, if you reject us now
we cannot fight alone.

ALL
7 How useless is all human help
when facing stubborn wrong!
But we shall triumph in the Lord,
and God shall be our song.

108B
From Psalm 108, Dale Garratt
© 1979 Scripture in Song/Thankyou Music

1 Through our God
      we shall do valiantly –
it is he who will tread down
      our enemies;
we'll sing and shout his victory:
   Christ is king!

2 For God has won the victory
and set his people free;
his word has slain the enemy,
the earth shall stand and see
      that through our God . . .
      Christ is king;
      Christ is king; Christ is king!

110
From Psalm 110
© Brian Foley

1 This is the word of God's decree,
the voice of God who ever is:
'I send my Son, true Son to me,
to make all kingdoms ever his!

2 'That City built for me of old,
his throne makes stronger, holier still;
the Reign of Justice, long foretold,
this Son of mine will there fulfil!

3 'A King to rule – my oath, my word! –
a greater King than kings before;
a Priest to pray – and will be heard! –
of highest Priesthood evermore;

4 'A Judge when earthly kingdoms fall,
to speak his verdict on their ways;
and then my Son, the King of all,
will bring to me his Kingdom's praise!'

111A
From Psalm 111
© Barbara Woollett/Jubilate Hymns

1 God's holy ways are just and true,
his promises are ever new,
   O praise him, alleluia!
Let every heart with praises sing
and make this house with voices ring;

O praise him, O praise him!
Alleluia, alleluia, alleluia!

2 Bring back to mind his grace and love,
our needs provided from above;
    O praise him, alleluia!
He kept his word, and Jesus came
to make a people for his name;
    O praise him, O praise him . . .

3 Tell once again his deeds of old,
the story of our mighty God,
    O praise him, alleluia!
For all his glorious works and ways
we shall rejoice through endless days;
    O praise him, O praise him . . .

111B
From Psalm 111
© Christopher Idle/Jubilate Hymns

1 Hallelujah, praise the Lord!
Where the people love his name,
where my Saviour is adored,
thanks and praise shall be my theme.
All his works are just and great;
here we find our chief delight:
good it is to meditate
all his everlasting right.

2 We recall what he has done,
tender mercies, firm and sure;
he is God, the holy One,
all his promises endure.
He provides our daily bread,
he defends his people's cause,
life and home and all we need,
by his everlasting laws.

3 Rich in his redeeming grace,
keeping covenant he came:
see the glory in his face –
holy, holy is his name!
Fear him – that is wisdom's way;
here begin our happiest days.
Trust him – thus we shall obey
God our everlasting praise.

111L
Psalm 111.1–10
© Editor/Jubilate Hymns

Praise the Lord:
praise the Lord!

With my whole heart I will thank the
Lord: in the company of his people.
Great are the works of the Lord:
A **those who wonder, seek them.**

Glorious and majestic are his deeds:
B **his goodness lasts for ever.**

He reminds us of his works of grace:
A **he is merciful and kind.**

He sustains those who fear him:
B **he keeps his covenant always.**

All he does is right and just:
A **all his words are faithful.**

They will last for ever and ever:
B **and be kept in faith and truth.**

He provided redemption for his people,
and made an eternal covenant with them:
ALL **holy and awesome is his name!**

The fear of the Lord is the beginning of
wisdom; he gives understanding to those
who obey:
to God belongs eternal praise!

**Glory to the Father, and to the Son,
and to the Holy Spirit:
as it was in the beginning, is now,
and shall be for ever. Amen.**

The congregation may divide at A *and* B.

112
From Psalm 112
© Michael Perry/Jubilate Hymns

1 How blessed are those who live by faith,
delighting in God's sure command;
for rich in grace will be their homes,
their children mighty in the land:

2 How happy those who freely give,
who justly deal and kindly care;
for in their darkness light shall dawn,
and long shall be their memory here:

3 How joyful those who, strong for truth,
rely upon the Lord most high;
unlike the wicked they shall live,
and lift their heads up to the sky!

4 Then praise the Lord – let joyful praise
to Father, Spirit, Son be given;
to God who loved us, came to save
and fills our hearts
    with grace from heaven!

113A
From Psalm 113
© Timothy Dudley-Smith

1 Servants of the living Lord,
bend in awe before his throne,
tell his majesty abroad,
know and name him God alone.
    Join to praise the Lord of grace,
    all who stand before his face.

2   Age to age, his name be blessed,
    Ancient of eternal days.
    Furthest bounds of east and west
    echo his perpetual praise:
      everliving Lord of grace,
      throned beyond all time and space.

3   Who like him in glory reigns
    higher than the heavens are high?
    He who world on world sustains,
    sun and stars and sea and sky:
      he it is who, Lord of grace,
      hears from heaven, his dwelling-place.

4   Lord of grace! In him we trust;
    by his love the lost are found,
    lowly lifted from the dust,
    happy homes with children crowned.
      All who stand before his face,
      praise, O praise, the Lord of grace!

113B   From Psalm 113, Paul Deming
              © 1976 copyright controlled

From the rising of the sun
to its going down
the Lord's name is to be praised;
from the rising . . .

Praise to the Lord;
praise him, all you servants of the Lord,
praise the name of the Lord!
Blessed be the name of the Lord
from this time forth
and for evermore!

113L   Psalm 113.1–9
              © Editor/Jubilate Hymns

A Praise the Lord:
   praise the Lord!

B You servants of the Lord, praise his
   name:
   **let the name of the Lord be praised,
   both now and for evermore!**

A From the rising of the sun to the place
   where it sets:
   the name of the Lord be praised!

B The Lord is exalted above the earth:
   his glory over the heavens.

A Who is like the Lord our God?
   He is throned in the heights above –

B Yet he bends down:
   yet he stoops to look at our world.

A He raises the poor from the dust:
   and lifts the needy from their sorrow.

B He honours the childless wife in her
   home:
   **he makes her happy,
   the mother of children.**

BOTH Praise the Lord:
      Amen.

The ministers/leaders may divide at A *and* B.

114   From Psalm 114
            © David Mowbray/Jubilate Hymns

1   When Israel broke their cruel chains
    and Egypt lost the day,
    the Lord's own people sang for joy
    and laughed upon their way.

2   When Israel crossed the river's edge
    and reached the promised land,
    they felt in their deliverance
    the touch of God's good hand.

3   Now we,
       through Christ who goes before,
    stand firm on solid ground;
    we sing God's praise, and all the earth
    shall tremble at the sound.

115   From Psalm 115
            © Timothy Dudley-Smith

1   Not to us be glory given
    but to him who reigns above.
    Glory to the God of heaven
    for his faithfulness and love!
    What though unbelieving voices
    hear no word and see no sign,
    still in God my heart rejoices,
    working out his will divine.

2   Not what human fingers fashion,
    gold and silver, deaf and blind,
    dead to knowledge and compassion,
    having neither heart nor mind –
    lifeless gods, some yet adore them,
    nerveless hands and feet of clay;
    all become, who bow before them,
    lost indeed, and dead as they.

3   Not in them is hope of blessing –
    hope is in the living Lord!
    High and low, his name confessing,
    find in him their shield and sword;
    hope of all whose hearts revere him,
    God of Israel, still the same!
    God of Aaron! Those who fear him,
    he remembers them by name.

4 Not the dead, but we the living
   praise the Lord with all our powers;
   of his goodness freely giving –
   his is heaven; earth is ours.
   Not to us be glory given
   but to him who reigns above.
   Glory to the God of heaven,
   for his faithfulness and love!

116A
From Psalm 116
© Barbara Woollett/Jubilate Hymns

(Let love to love respond and say,
'O praise the Lord with me today!')

1 I love the Lord, he heard my voice,
   he listened when I called his name;
   in thankfulness I shall rejoice
   his grace and mercy to proclaim.
     Let love to love respond and say,
     'O praise the Lord with me today!'

2 When dark despair entangled me,
   in depths of grief I called his name;
   from sin and death he set me free,
   and to my rescue Jesus came.
     Let love to love . . .

3 I cried with sorrow many tears –
   in guilty dread I called his name;
   but God forgave my doubts and fears,
   he told me Jesus took the blame:
     Let love to love . . .

4 Now that I know he answers prayer,
   with child-like trust I'll call his name;
   when there is no one else to care
   his steadfast love will stay the same.
     Let love to love . . .

5 Turn to the Lord, his word obey,
   lift up your voice and call his name;
   ask him to lead you in his way –
   his promised love is yours to claim:
     Let love to love . . .

116B
From Psalm 116, © David Frost
Pointing © Wm Collins

**How can I repay the Lord
for all the goodness he shows to me?**

1 I love the Lord because he ' heard my '
   voice:
   the ' voice of · my ' suppli'cation;
2 because he in'clined his ' ear to me:
   in the ' day ' that I ' called to him.

3 The cords of death encompassed me *
   the snares of the ' grave took ' hold on
   me:
   I ' was in ' anguish · and ' sorrow.

4 Then I called upon the ' name · of the '
   Lord:
   **'O ' Lord · I be'seech you ·
   de'liver me!'**
     How can I repay . . .

5 Gracious and righteous ' is the ' Lord:
   full of com'passion ' is our ' God.
6 The Lord pre'serves the ' simple:
   **when ' I was · brought ' low
   he ' saved me.**
     How can I repay . . .

7 Return O my ' soul · to your ' rest:
   for the ' Lord ' has re'warded you.
8 For you O Lord have delivered my '
   soul from ' death:
   **my eyes from ' tears ·
   and my ' feet from ' falling.**
     How can I repay . . .

116L
Psalm 116.1–19
© Editor/Jubilate Hymns

I love the Lord because he heard my
voice:
A **the Lord
   in mercy listened to my prayers.**

Because the Lord has turned his ear to
me:
B **I'll call on him as long as I shall live.**

The cords of death entangled me around:
C **the horrors of the grave
   came over me.**

But then I called upon the Lord my God:
A **I said to him,
   'O Lord, I beg you, save!'**

The Lord our God is merciful and good:
B **the Lord protects
   the simple-hearted ones.**

The Lord saved me from death and
stopped my tears:
C **he saved me from defeat
   and picked me up.**

And so I walk before him all my days:
A **and live to love and praise
   his holy name.**

What shall I give the Lord for all his
grace?
B **I'll take his saving cup,
   and pay my vows.**

Within the congregation of his saints:
C **I'll offer him my sacrifice of praise.**

Praise the Lord:
ALL **Amen, amen!**

The congregation may divide at A, B and C.

117A
From Psalm 117
© Christopher Idle/Jubilate Hymns

Praise the Lord, all nations, praise;
worship God, all humankind:
  Alleluia, praise the Lord!
Mighty is your love for us,
firm for ever is your truth:
  Alleluia, praise the Lord!

117B
From Psalm 117, Jacques Berthier
© Taizé/Wm Collins

CONTINUOUS RESPONSE
  Praise him, you nations,
  praise him, you peoples;
  praise him, praise him,
  praise the Lord.

1 Praise the Lord, all you nations;
  praise him, all you peoples.
    Alleluia!
  Strong is his love and mercy;
  he is faithful for ever.
    Alleluia!

2 Alleluia, alleluia:
  let everything living
  give praise to the Lord.
  Alleluia, alleluia:
  let everything living
  give praise to the Lord.

117C
From Psalm 117
© Paul Inwood/Magnificat Music

LEADER Holy is God, holy and strong,
       God ever-living, alleluia!
  ALL Holy is God, holy and strong,
       God ever-living, alleluia!

1 Sing the Lord's praise, every nation,
  give him all honour and glory:
  strong is his love for his people;
  his faithfulness is eternal.
      Holy is God . . .

2 Praise to the Father almighty,
  praise to his Son, Christ the Lord,
  praise to the life-giving Spirit,
  both now and for ever. Amen.
      Holy is God . . .
      Holy is God . . .
      Holy is God . . .

117L
Psalm 117.1–2
© Editor/Jubilate Hymns

Praise the Lord, all you nations:
A **praise him, all you people!**

Great is his love towards us:
B **his faithfulness shall last for ever.**

Praise the Lord:
Amen.

The congregation may divide at A and B.

118A
From Psalm 118
© David Mowbray/Jubilate Hymns

1 Open the gates of righteousness,
  for we have come to pray;
  to offer thanks for all God's gifts
  within his house today.

2 When we were trapped at every turn,
  hard-pressed on every side,
  the Lord our God came to our help
  and all our bonds untied.

3 The rock the builders had refused
  became the corner-stone:
  who can deny this is a thing
  the Lord himself has done?

4 Enter God's house to praise his name,
  and all his triumphs tell;
  salute the people of the Lord –
  Beloved, we wish you well!

118B
From Psalm 118
Author unknown

This is the day, this is the day,
that the Lord has made,
    that the Lord has made;
we will rejoice, we will rejoice,
and be glad in it, and be glad in it:
  This is the day
  that the Lord has made,
  we will rejoice and be glad in it;
  this is the day, this is the day
  that the Lord has made.

118L
Psalm 118.1–29
© Editor/Jubilate Hymns

M Give thanks to the Lord, for he is good:
  his love endures for ever.

M All those who fear the Lord shall say:
  His love endures for ever.

W Open for me the gates of the temple; I
  will go in and give thanks to the Lord.

M This is the gate of the Lord, only the righteous can come in.

W I will give thanks because you heard me; you have become my salvation.

C The stone which the builders rejected as worthless turned out to be the most important of all:

ALL **The Lord has done this –
what a wonderful sight it is!**

W This is the day of the Lords's victory – let us be happy, let us celebrate:

ALL **O Lord save us –
O Lord, grant us success.**

M May God bless the one who comes in the name of the Lord:

ALL **The Lord is God –
he has been good to us!**

C From the temple of the Lord, we bless you.

D With branches in your hands, start the procession and march round the altar:

W You are my God and I will give you thanks:

ALL **You are my God, and I will exalt you.**

M Give thanks to the Lord, for he is good:
his love endures for ever. Amen.

M – minister, W – worshipper – from doorway, then moving through congregation, C – choir/chorus, D – director – in matter-of-fact tone.

119A

From Psalm 119
© Timothy Dudley-Smith

1 The will of God to mark my way,
    the word of God for light;
  eternal justice to obey
    in everlasting right.

2 Your eyes of mercy keep me still,
    your gracious love be mine;
  so work in me your perfect will
    and cause your face to shine.

3 With ordered step secure and strong,
    from sin's oppression freed,
  redeemed from every kind of wrong
    in thought and word and deed –

4 So set my heart to love your word
    and every promise prove,
  to walk with truth before the Lord
    in righteousness and love.

119B

From Psalm 119
© David Mowbray/Jubilate Hymns

1 With all my heart I seek
    the true and living way!
  Lord, guide these steps of mine
    or I shall go astray.

2 Let me not waver now
    from simple honesty,
  or fail in my resolve
    to keep integrity.

3 Your laws and your commands
    remain my great delight;
  I speak of them at noon
    and ponder them at night.

4 Through youth and through old age,
    Lord, may I not forget
  that in your matchless word,
    there love and truth have met.

119C

From Psalm 119, © David Frost
Pointing © Wm Collins

Blessed are those whose | way is | blameless:
who | walk · in the | law · of the | Lord.
**Blessed are those who | keep ·
his com|mands:
and seek him |
with their | whole | heart.**

I have treasured your | words · in my | heart:
that I | might not | sin a|gainst you.
**Blessed are | you Lord | God:
O | teach me | your | statutes.**

With my lips I | have been | telling: all the | judgements | of your | mouth;
**and I find more joy
in the way of | your com|mands:
than in | all | manner · of | riches.**

Guide me in the path of | your com|mandments: for there|in is | my de|light.
**The law of your mouth
is | dearer · to | me:
than a | wealth of | gold and | silver.**

Lord how I | love your | law: it is my medi|tation | all the · day | long.
**How sweet are your | words ·
to my | tongue:
sweeter than | honey | to my | mouth.**

Your word is a lantern ' to my ' feet: and
a ' light ' to my ' path.
**Your commands are my in'heritance ·
for ' ever:**
they ' are the ' joy of · my ' heart.

Glory to the Father and ' to the ' Son:
and ' to the ' Holy ' Spirit;
as it was in the be'ginning · is ' now:
and shall be for ' ever. 'A'men.

119D
From Psalm 119
© Christopher Idle/Jubilate Hymns

1 All your commandments, Father almighty,
Bring to your children
     healing and blessing;
Christians who keep them
     find here their comfort.

2 Daily instruct us as your disciples:
Each of your statutes stands firm for ever;
Faithful your promise,
     full your forgiveness.

3 God of all mercy,
     grant me your guidance;
How can a young man keep his way holy?
I have found treasure in your instruction.

4 Joy comes to nations
     knowing your judgements;
Keeping them
     brings us close to your kingdom –
Laws that spell freedom, true liberation.

5 My heart is listening for you
     each morning;
Never desert me; speak in the night-time;
Open my eyes, Lord,
     then lead me onwards.

6 Put right my passions
     by your clear precepts;
Quell my rebellions, rescue me quickly;
Raise and restore me, mighty Redeemer.

7 Saviour
     whose Spirit gave us the Scriptures,
Train me to trust them
     when I am tempted;
Unless you helped me, I would go under.

8 Vain are my own ways;
     yours is the victory;
Wonderful Counsellor,
     you are my wisdom;
Your word shall teach me;
     I will obey you.

119E
From Psalm 119, Amy Grant
© 1983 Bug and Bear Music

Your word is a lamp unto my feet
and a light unto my path;
your word is a lamp unto my feet
and a light unto my path.

1 When I feel afraid, think I've lost my way,
still you're there right beside me:
and nothing will I fear
as long as you are near.
Please be near me to the end.
     Your word . . .

2 I will not forget your love for me –
     and yet
my heart for ever is wandering:
Jesus, be my guide
and hold me to your side.
And I will love you to the end.
     Your word . . .

119F
From Psalm 119
© Roger Mayor/Jubilate Hymns

ALL
Show me how much you love me, Lord,
and save me
     according to your promise;
show me how much you love me, Lord,
and save me
     according to your promise.

SOLO
1 Teach me, Lord,
     the meaning of your laws
and I will obey them at all times.
ALL Show me how much . . .

SOLO
2 I will live in perfect freedom
because I try to obey your laws.
ALL Show me how much . . .

SOLO
3 Even in my suffering I was comforted
because your promise gave me life.
ALL Show me how much . . .

121A
From Psalm 121
© Brian Foley

1 I see the mountains far away,
the borders of the world I know,
where God, it seems, must live alone
in places where I may not go!

2 I look beyond familiar things,
beyond the limits set for me,
to where, it seems, God hides himself,
too far, too deep, in secrecy!

3 Yet God is present where I am,
  a hidden God, though ever near,
  not one who lives and loves alone,
  but God, my God, who loves me here.

4 My place in history and my name,
  my years, my days, and all they bring –
  in these I see God's will for me,
  his love for me, in everything.

121B
From Psalm 121
© Timothy Dudley-Smith

1 I lift my eyes
  to the quiet hills
  in the press of a busy day;
    as green hills stand
    in a dusty land
  so God is my strength and stay.

2 I lift my eyes
  to the quiet hills
  to a calm that is mine to share;
    secure and still
    in the Father's will
  and kept by the Father's care.

3 I lift my eyes
  to the quiet hills
  with a prayer as I turn to sleep;
    by day, by night,
    through the dark and light
  my Shepherd will guard his sheep.

4 I lift my eyes
  to the quiet hills
  and my heart to the Father's throne;
    in all my ways
    to the end of days
  the Lord will preserve his own.

121C
From Psalm 121
Mark Pallant and Steven Brazier
© 1987 Ears and Eyes Music Ltd/
Boosey & Hawkes Music Publishers Ltd

  I will lift up my eyes to the hills –
  oh where shall I find my help?
  My help will come from the Lord,
  the maker of heaven and earth.

1 He will not let your foot slip,
  he who guards you will not slumber;
  he who watches over Israel
  will neither slumber nor sleep.
    I will lift up my eyes . . .

2 The Lord, he is your guardian,
  the Lord is your defence
      at your right hand;
  the sun will not harm you by day
  nor the moon by night.
    I will lift up my eyes . . .

3 The Lord will protect you
      from all danger,
  he will watch over your life;
  the Lord will guard your coming
      and your going,
  both now and for evermore.
    I will lift up my eyes to the hills –
    oh where shall I find my help?
    My help will come from the Lord,
    the maker of heaven,
    the maker of heaven,
    the maker of heaven and earth.

121D
Psalm 121, © David Frost
Pointing © Wm Collins

1 I lift up my ' eyes · to the ' hills:
  but ' where · shall I ' find ' help?
2 My help ' comes · from the ' Lord:
  who has ' made ' heaven · and ' earth.

3 He will not suffer your ' foot to ' stumble:
  **and he who watches ' over · you '
  will not ' sleep.**
4 Be sure he who has ' charge of ' Israel:
  will ' neither ' slumber · nor ' sleep.

5 The Lord him'self is · your ' keeper:
  **the Lord is your defence
    up'on your ' right ' hand;**
6 the sun shall not ' strike you · by ' day:
  nor ' shall the ' moon by ' night.

7 The Lord will defend you from ' all ' evil:
  it is ' he · who will ' guard your ' life.
8 The Lord will defend your going out and
  your ' coming ' in:
  **from this time ' forward ·
  for ' ever'more.**

  **Glory to the Father and ' to the ' Son:
  and ' to the ' Holy ' Spirit;
  as it was in the be'ginning · is ' now:
  and shall be for ' ever. ' A'men.**

121E
From Psalm 121
© Pearl Beasley/Jubilate Hymns

1 When I look towards the hills,
  I know God's help is there;
  he will keep me from all ills
  through his own loving care.

2 He will shield me from all harm
  each minute of the day;
  and the stress of life he'll calm –
  for by my side he'll stay.

3 Day nor night no hurt will bring –
  his help is always here;
  he will guide through everything,
  whose love is ever near.

121F

From Psalm 121, Bill Batstone
© 1984 Maranatha! Music/Word Music (UK)

1 I look up to the mountains,
    to the hills I turn my eyes:
who will come to help me,
    can I find a place to hide?
The One who made the heavens
    and the earth will hear my call,
the Lord will come to help me
    and he will not let me fall.
He will not let you fall,
    he will not let you fall;
    he is never weary,
    and he will not let you fall.
    He will not . . .

2 The One who watches Israel
    will his vigil keep,
through the burning sunlight
    and in the darkness deep;
constantly beside you –
    you need not fear at all,
the Lord is there to help you,
    and he will not let you fall.
    He will not . . .

3 So when you are in danger,
    when by trouble you are found,
and your very soul is threatened
    by the evil all around;
in all of your ways and
    in your troubles great and small,
now and ever after
    he will not let you fall.
    He will not . . .

121G

From Psalm 121, Phil Potter
© 1985 Ears and Eyes Music Ltd/
Boosey & Hawkes Music Publishers Ltd

1 I'll lift my eyes to the hills,
I'll lift my eyes to the hills;
I'll lift my eyes to worship God,
I'll lift my eyes to the hills.

2 I'll bring my praise to the Lord . . .

3 Lift up your voice to the Lord . . .

4 We lift our hands to the Lord . . .

5 We lift our hearts to the King . . .

121H

From Psalm 121, Malcolm Scott
© 1987 Ears and Eyes Music Ltd/
Boosey & Hawkes Music Publishers Ltd

I will lift up my eyes,
I will lift up my eyes,
to the glory and the majesty of God.
I will lift up my eyes . . .

I will lift up my eyes
to see the mountains round about,
to remind me of the majesty of God:
for the Lord who made the mountains
and the rivers in the valleys
is the Lord who leads his people
    by his word.
    I will lift up my eyes . . .

122A

From Psalm 122
© Basil Bridge

1 I rejoiced to hear them say,
    'Come and worship God today!
Come, with heart and mind and soul,
    seek the peace that makes us whole;
see disordered lives restored
    in the presence of the Lord:
from your burdens find release;
    in his presence there is peace.'

2 Here in gratitude we bring
    all we are to serve our King;
his forgiveness we entreat
    in whom love and justice meet:
bring our needs to him in prayer,
    ask his help, and trust his care;
join with all, in every place,
    who have sought and known his grace.

3 God, the Lord of peace, is near –
    come in faith, and meet him here;
let each restless soul be still,
    glad to know and do his will:
as a city's walls and towers
    offered safety – God is ours!
Therefore we rejoice, and say,
    'Come and worship God today!'

122B

From Psalm 122
© Christopher Idle/Jubilate Hymns

1 Jerusalem! How glad I was
    when they invited me
to climb with them the mount of prayer,
    the place of majesty:
Jerusalem! Within your gates
    our willing feet have stood,
and there we raised our voices high
    to fill the house of God.

2 Jerusalem! A city built
    compact and walled around;
the sacred tribes ascended here
    and made their psalms resound.
Let us, like Israel, go up
    to pay the Lord our dues,
to hear the judgements of the law,
    the joy of God's good news.

3 Jerusalem! May you have peace,
   your people long endure;
   may all your citizens be safe,
   your towers and streets secure.
   For brothers, sisters, friends, I pray
   let peace return again:
   O Lord our God, meet us in grace,
   in glory come to reign!

122c
From Psalm 122
© Norman Warren/Jubilate Hymns

I was glad when they said to me
let us go to the house of the Lord:
here we are in the presence of God,
giving thanks to our mighty Lord.

DURING REPEAT VERSE
Pray for peace,
pray for peace,
pray for peace for the city of God:
Peace be with you, peace be with you;
peace be with you, peace be with you!

122d
From Psalm 122
© International Bible Society

Let us go to the house of the Lord.

1 I rejoiced with those who said to me,
   'Let us go to the house of the Lord'.
   Our feet are standing in your gates,
   Jerusalem, like a city built together,
   where the people of God go up,
   to praise the name of the Lord.
   Let us go to the house of the Lord.

2 For peace for all Jerusalem,
   and loved ones – this we pray:
   let people be secure
       where they must live
   and to all my friends and family –
   May God's peace be within you,
   for the sake of the house of the Lord.

122e
From Psalm 122
© this version David Preston/Jubilate Hymns

1 What joy to hear the pilgrims say,
   'Will you come up with us,
   to keep the Lord's appointed feast
   and worship at his house?'

2 Within the city gates we stand,
   amazed as now we see
   Jerusalem's complete design,
   her perfect unity.

MEN
3 There to give praise and thanks to God
   the ransomed tribes resort;
   there David's son in judgement sits
   and holds his royal court.

WOMEN
4 May peace abide within her walls,
   prosperity abound,
   with every good and perfect gift
   her people all be crowned!

ALL
5 So for Jerusalem I'll pray
   while life and breath remain,
   since there my friends and kindred dwell
   and God shall ever reign.

122l
Psalm 122.1–8
© Editor/Jubilate Hymns

I was glad when they said to me:
let us go to the house of the Lord!

Pray for the peace of Jerusalem:
A **may those who love our land
   be blessed.**

May there be peace in your homes:
B **and safety for our families.**

For the sake of those we love we say:
Let there be peace! Amen.

**Glory to the Father, and to the Son,
and to the Holy Spirit:
as it was in the beginning, is now,
and shall be for ever. Amen.**

The congregation may divide at A – *male
voices, and* B – *female voices.*

123a
From Psalm 123
© Christopher Idle/Jubilate Hymns

1 I lift my eyes to you,
   to heaven your royal throne:
   as servants watch their master's hand
   we look to you alone.

2 Have mercy, Lord, we pray,
   and hear your people's cries:
   until your mercy reaches us
   on you we fix our eyes.

3 The proud have mocked us long,
   their scorn we have endured;
   our days are filled with their contempt:
   we look to you, O Lord.

123B
From Psalm 123
© David Mowbray/Jubilate Hymns

1 Master, we lift
    our eyes, expecting
your promised gift,
    your arm protecting:
though some have lied,
    our faith despising –
you are our guide,
    resting and rising.

2 Trinity strong,
    source of all blessing:
joyful our song,
    worship expressing;
Father and Son,
    Spirit life-giver:
your will be done,
    now and for ever.

123C
From Psalm 123, Jacques Berthier
© 1978, 1980 and 1981 Taizé/Wm Collins

CONTINUOUS RESPONSE – ALL
Holy Lord, have mercy on us all,
Lord have mercy on us;
Holy Lord . . .
OR:
Miserere nobis Domine,
miserere nobis;
miserere nobis Domine,
miserere nobis.

SOLO
1 Behold, as the eyes of servants
are on the hands of their masters:
ALL Holy Lord . . .
ALL *Miserere . . .*

SOLO
2 Our eyes are fixed on the Lord our God
until he shows us his mercy.
ALL Holy Lord . . .
ALL *Miserere . . .*

124A
From Psalm 124
© Paul Wigmore/Jubilate Hymns

1 If the Lord had not been near,
at our side and quick to hear,
who would then have calmed our fear?
    Let us praise the Lord!

2 If the Lord had not come in,
strong to save from deadly sin,
who would then have helped us win?
    Let us praise the Lord!

3 If the Lord who set us free
did not hear us, could not see,
who would then our saviour be?
    Let us praise the Lord!

4 Swift and certain to our aid
comes the one by whom were made
starry heavens, woodland glade.
    Let us praise the Lord!

124B
From Psalm 124
© International Bible Society

If the Lord had not been on our side
would we still be here today;
and if the Lord had not been on our side,
would we not be swept away?
    But like a bird,
    like a bird out from the net
    we have broken free;
    but like a bird,
    like a bird out from the net
    we have broken free.

If the Lord . . .
But like a bird . . .

    (*Instrumental*)

But like a bird . . .
. . . we have broken free,
we have broken free,
we have broken free.

124L
Psalm 124.1–8
© Editor/Jubilate Hymns

If the Lord had not been on our side –
now let Israel say:
If the Lord had not been on our side –
A **when enemies attacked us,**
B **when their anger flared against us,**
C **they would have swallowed us alive.**
A **The flood would have engulfed us,**
B **the torrent would have swept over us,**
C **the waters would have drowned us.**

Praise the Lord:
A **who has not given us up to their teeth.**
B **We have escaped**
like a bird from the snare:
C **the snare is broken and we are free.**

Our help is in the name of the Lord:
ALL **who made heaven and earth. Amen.**

The congregation may divide at A, B and C.

125 From Psalm 125
© Christopher Idle/Jubilate Hymns

1 Those who rely on the Lord
      are unshakeable,
  firm as mount Zion, supremely assured;
  just as the mountains encircle Jerusalem,
  round us forever is standing the Lord.

2 Evil shall not always rule
      over righteousness,
  God's time will come
      when oppression shall cease:
  Lord, bless the righteous,
      restrain the impenitent,
  grant to your people
      the gift of your peace.

126A From Psalm 126
© David Mowbray/Jubilate Hymns

1 Laughter and song!
  The Lord has done great things:
  his people once were freed
  from tyrant kings.

2 Yet now we wait
  in sad captivity:
  rise up, redeeming Lord,
  to set us free!

3 Tears turn to joy!
  The weeping farmer sows
  and, slowly through the storms,
  the harvest grows.

126B Psalm 126, © David Frost
Pointing © Wm Collins

1 When the Lord turned again the ˈ
  fortunes · of ˈ Zion:
  then were we
      like ˈ men reˈstored to ˈ life.
2 Then was our mouth ˈ filled with ˈ
  laughter:
      and ˈ our ˈ tongue with ˈ singing.
3 Then said they aˈmong the ˈ heathen:
  'The Lord
      has ˈ done great ˈ things for ˈ them.'
4 Truly the Lord has done great ˈ things
  for ˈ us:
      and ˈ therefore ˈ we reˈjoiced.
5 Turn again our ˈ fortunes · O ˈ Lord:
      as the streams reˈturn ·
      to the ˈ dry ˈ south.
6 Those that ˈ sow in ˈ tears:
      shall ˈ reap with ˈ songs of ˈ joy.

Second part
7 He who goes out weeping * ˈ bearing ·
  the ˈ seed:
      shall come again in gladness ˈ
      bringing · his ˈ sheaves ˈ with him.

  Glory to the Father and ˈ to the ˈ Son:
  and ˈ to the ˈ Holy ˈ Spirit;
  as it was in the beˈginning · is ˈ now:
  and shall be for ˈ ever. ˈ Aˈmen.

126C From Psalm 126
© Michael Saward/Jubilate Hymns

1 When God delivered Israel
  from bondage long ago,
  they thought that they were dreaming,
  but soon they turned to laughing
      and sang the song of joy,
      and sang the song of joy.

2 The godless nations round them
  could not deny his power;
  they cried, 'O see this marvel!'
  'God's work!' replied his people;
      and so they sang for joy,
      and so they sang for joy.

3 O God, restore our nation;
  come irrigate dry souls,
  that those who sow in sadness
  may reap their sheaves with gladness,
      and sing the song of joy,
      and sing the song of joy!

126D From Psalm 126
© John McNeil

  Sound on the trumpet,
  call to the people,
  sing your new song –
  our Bridegroom's coming,
  it won't be long.

  Break out the banners,
  join in the dancing,
  no time for gloom –
  prepare the banquet,
  he's coming soon.

1 If you're one of God's people,
  rejoice in praise and song;
  come lift up your hearts before him
  and give your voices in praise and song.
      Sound on the trumpet . . .

2   Go out with tears and weeping
    to bring the harvest home:
    it's time for the joy of reaping;
    in joy the sheaves now are coming home.
     Sound on the trumpet . . .

     Yes!

126E
From Psalm 126, Doug Constable
© 1978 Thankyou Music

1   When the Lord, he turned again
    the wretchedness of Zion;
    then we laughed and sang for joy
    as children of the dream,
    then we laughed and sang for joy
    as children of the dream.

2   Then they said, the heathen said,
    'The Lord has done great things!'
    Yes, he's done great things for us –
    in him we now rejoice;
    yes, he's done great things for us –
    in him we now rejoice.

3   When the Lord, he turned again
    the wretchedness of Zion;
    then we laughed and sang for joy
    as children of the dream,
    then we laughed and sang for joy
    as children of the dream.

126L
Psalm 126.1–6
© Editor/Jubilate Hymns

    When the Lord brought us back from
    slavery:
A **we were like those who dream.**

    Our mouths were filled with laughter;
B **our tongues with songs of joy.**

    Then those around us said, 'The Lord has
    done great things for them':
A **The Lord has done great things for us,
   and we are filled with joy.**

    Those who sow in tears
B **shall reap with songs of joy.**

    **Glory to the Father, and to the Son,
   and to the Holy Spirit:
   as it was in the beginning, is now,
   and shall be for ever. Amen.**

The congregation may divide at A *and* B, *in
which case the* Gloria *should be used.*

127A
From Psalms 127 and 124
© Brian Foley

1   If God is building when we build,
    the house we raise will stand;
    if God designs when we design,
    his skill is in our hand:

2   If God is guarding when we guard,
    he keeps the watch we keep,
    protects our ways, provides our days
    the harvest that we reap:

3   If God is working when we work
    to make the things we make;
    he gives approval and success
    to labour for his sake:

4   If God is speaking when we speak,
    our words become his word,
    and in the speech of everyday,
    eternal things are heard:

5   If God is building when we build,
    we call each work our own,
    but not for us to praise ourselves –
    our praise is God alone!

127B
From Psalm 127
© David Mowbray/Jubilate Hymns

1   Unless the Lord has built the house
    it must be built again;
    except the Lord defends a town
    its watchmen wake in vain.

2   What value has a life of haste,
    of endless, anxious toil?
    God has for those who keep his law
    a garland none can spoil:

3   Among God's gifts, a happy home –
    a blessing rich indeed;
    a joyful, loving partnership,
    a strength to those in need.

4   That home, that house, as years go by
    must weather storm and strain:
    unless the Lord has built the house
    it must be built again.

127C
From Psalm 127
© Mollie Knight/Jubilate Hymns

1   Unless the Lord constructs the house,
    the builders work in vain;
    the Lord alone designs and builds
    foundations that remain.

2   Unless the Lord is keeping watch
    the city cannot stand;
    the sentry guards the gates in vain
    without God's mighty hand.

3 In vain you labour night and day,
by constant care oppressed;
the Lord supplies his loved ones' needs
and grants them sleep and rest.

4 The Lord designed the family,
providing earthly love;
our children are his heritage –
a gift from heaven above.

5 Like weapons in a warrior's hand
are those who bear our name;
with them we face a hostile world
assured, and free from shame.

128A
From Psalm 128
© Christopher Idle/Jubilate Hymns

1 Blessed are those who fear the Lord,
walking in God's perfect ways;
all they do shall bring reward,
love enriches all their days.

2 Blessings greet the husband, wife,
parents, children, old and young;
fruits of faith be theirs for life,
joy in songs together sung.

3 Bless us, Lord! Your kingdom come;
children's children learn your praise:
prayer in nation, church and home,
peace in Christ to crown our days.

128B
From Psalm 128
© David Mowbray/Jubilate Hymns

1 Bless all who trust in God
and walk within God's ways;
bless every soul whose happiness
springs from the Lord's own praise!

2 Let marriages be strong
and sparkle bright as wine;
let partners and let children thrive
and flourish like the vine!

3 And since we may not boast
such joys are ours by right,
teach us, good Lord, to take your gifts
with thanks and with delight.

128C
From Psalm 128
© The Grail/AP Watt Ltd

O blessed are those
who fear the Lord
and walk in his ways;
O blessed are those
who fear the Lord
and walk in his ways!

1 O blessed are those who fear the Lord
and walk in his ways!
By the labour of your hands
you shall eat –
you will be happy and prosper.
O blessed are those . . .

2 Your wife like a fruitful vine
in the heart of your house;
your children like shoots of the olive
around your table:
O blessed are those . . .

3 Indeed, thus shall be blessed
all those who fear the Lord:
may the Lord bless you from Zion
all the days of your life!
O blessed are those . . .

128L
Psalm 128.1–6
© Editor/Jubilate Hymns

The pilgrims' song:
A **Blessed are those who fear the Lord,**
B **who walk in his ways.**

You will eat the fruit of your work;
blessings and prosperity will be yours:
A **Blessed are those who fear the Lord,**
B **who walk in his ways.**

Your wife will be like a fruitful vine
within your house; your children will be
like young olive trees around your table:
A **Blessed are those who fear the Lord,**
B **who walk in his ways.**

May the Lord bless you all the days of
your life; may you have prosperity; may
you live to see your children's children:
ALL **Peace be with you. Amen.**

The congregation may divide at A *and* B.

130A
From Psalm 130, Fred Kaan
© Stainer & Bell Ltd

1 Out of our failure to create
a world of love and care;
out of the depths of human life
we cry to God in prayer.

2 Out of the darkness of our time,
of days for ever gone,
our souls are longing for the light,
like watchmen for the dawn.

3 Out of the depths we cry to him
whose will is strong and just;
all human hole-and-corner ways
are by his light exposed.

4 Hope in the Lord whose timeless love
  gives laughter where we wept;
  the Father, who at every point
  his word has given and kept.

130B
From Psalm 130
© Christopher Idle/Jubilate Hymns

1 Up from the depths I cry to God:
  O listen, Lord, to me;
  O hear my voice in this distress,
  this mire of misery.
    I wait for God with all my heart,
    my hope is in his word;
    and more than watchmen for the dawn
    I'm longing for the Lord.

2 If you, my God, should measure guilt
  who then could ever stand?
  But those who fear your name will find
  forgiveness from your hand.
    I wait for God . . .

3 O Israel, set your hope on God
  whose mercy is supreme:
  the nation mourning for its sin
  he surely will redeem.
    I wait for God . . .

130C
From Psalm 130
© David Mowbray/Jubilate Hymns

1 Out of the depths I cry:
  O God, remember me!
  What earthly help have I
  if you watch silently?

2 If you watch silently
  and mark things done amiss,
  to whom then may I fly
  at such a time as this?

3 At such a time as this
  my soul waits for the Lord;
  no joy is there, no bliss
  without his saving word.

4 Without his saving word,
  all hope for ever dies:
  speak now, most mighty Lord,
  and from the depths I rise!

130D
From Psalm 130
© David Preston/Jubilate Hymns

1 From deep despair to you I call:
  Lord, hear me when I cry!
  O turn your ear to hear my voice
  which pleads with you on high!

2 O Lord, if you record our sins,
  who ever could be spared?
  But mercy may be found with you,
  that you may then be feared.

3 Now for the Lord my spirit waits,
  my hope is in his word;
  more than the watchmen wait for dawn
  my soul waits for the Lord.

4 O Israel, hope in God the Lord!
  His grace is full and free,
  and pays the price to ransom us
  from all iniquity.

130E
From Psalm 130
© David Mowbray/Jubilate Hymns

1 From the very depths I cry:
    Lord, hear my voice,
  in your mercy, pass not by,
    Lord, hear my voice;
  let your ears consider well,
  Lord, the hope of Israel,
  save my soul from utmost hell.
    Lord, hear my voice!

2 In your word I put my trust:
    Lord, hear my voice,
  lift my spirit from the dust,
    Lord, hear my voice;
  prayer awakens with the dawning,
  from the watch before the morning:
  always patient, never scorning
    Lord, hear my voice!

130F
From Psalm 130, Bill Batstone
© 1986 Maranatha! Music/Word Music (UK)

1 I call to you from out of the deep,
  O Lord, most high;
  aware of my sin and the distance I keep
  from the Light, O Lord.
    But there is forgiveness with you!
    In wonder I fall on my knees;
    my soul waits for the Lord
    in the hope of his promise –
    in the hope of his promise
    deliverance will come.
    My soul waits for the Lord
    through the night to the morning,
    like a night-watchman waiting
    for the coming of the dawn.

2 Look to the Lord all you people in need,
  for he is kind;
  he will break
      the chains of your soul's slavery –
  for all time, O Lord.
    But there is forgiveness . . .

3 Tell me who could stand
in the Lord's righteous reckoning
if our lives faced his light?
Then, if all our deeds were revealed
at God's beckoning,
who could hold their head high?
But there is forgiveness with you!
In wonder I fall on my knees;
my soul waits for the Lord
in the hope of his promise –
in the hope of his promise
deliverance will come.
My soul waits for the Lord
through the night to the morning,
like a night-watchman waiting
for the coming of the dawn.

130G
From Psalm 130, Jacques Berthier
© 1982, 1983 and 1984 Taizé/Wm Collins

O Lord, hear my prayer;
O Lord, hear my prayer:
when I call, answer me –
O Lord, hear my prayer;
O Lord, hear my prayer;
come and listen to me.

O Lord . . .

131A
From Psalm 131
© Stephen Horsfall/Jubilate Hymns

1 Before the Lord my soul is bowed
in trust and quiet humility;
I do not let my heart grow proud
or ponder things too great for me.

2 But I have made my spirit calm;
my soul is like a child at rest
who knows that it is safe from harm
and sleeps upon its mother's breast.

3 Let grateful voices tell abroad
the mighty name that we adore:
O Israel, hope in God the Lord,
your glory now and evermore!

131B
From Psalm 131
© David Mowbray/Jubilate Hymns

1 Lord, this thing I ask you:
hold in check my pride,
as a child obedient
at its mother's side.

2 All God's sons and daughters
to his heart are dear:
let them now and always
trust, and never fear.

132
From Psalm 132
© David Mowbray/Jubilate Hymns

1 As David took no rest until
he housed the ark secure,
so in the working of God's will
may we by faith endure.

2 As David trusted God to set
an heir upon his throne,
so may God's people never doubt
that justice will be done.

3 Arise, O Lord, and come today
in your great power and might;
crown all your chosen ones with joy
and lead us into light!

133A
From Psalm 133, J E Seddon
© Mrs M Seddon/Jubilate Hymns

1 How good a thing it is,
how pleasant to behold,
when all God's people live at one,
the law of love uphold!

2 As perfume, by its scent,
breathes fragrance all around,
so life itself will sweeter be
where unity is found.

3 And like refreshing dew
that falls upon the hills,
true union sheds its gentle grace,
and deeper love instils.

4 God grants the choicest gifts
to those who live in peace;
to them such blessings shall abound
and evermore increase.

133B
From Psalm 133
© Keith Landis

1 Behold how pleasant it shall be
for those who dwell in unity
as children of the Lord;
though not by nature so inclined,
they have in Christ one heart and mind,
miraculous accord!

2 Like precious oil poured on each head,
like dew upon mount Zion shed,
his mercies freely flow;
and even more, the Lord commands
the fairest blessing of his hands –
eternal life to know!

134A

From Psalm 134, *Come bless the Lord*
© Timothy Dudley-Smith

1 Bless the Lord as day departs;
   let your lamps be brightly burning,
   lifting holy hands and hearts
   to the Lord, till day's returning.

2 As within the darkened shrine,
   faithful to their sacred calling,
   sons and priests of Levi's line
   blessed the Lord as night was falling:

3 So may we who watch or rest
   bless the Lord of earth and heaven;
   and by him ourselves be blessed,
   grace and peace and mercy given.

134B

From Psalm 134, *Come bless the Lord*
© Christopher Idle/Jubilee Hymns

1 Come, praise the Lord,
       all you his servants
   who stand within his house by night;
   come lift your hands and hearts
       in worship,
   God be your praise and your delight.

2 Come, bless the Lord,
       all those who love him,
   who serve within the holy place;
   may God who made
       both earth and heaven
   grant us the blessings of his grace.

134C

From Psalm 134, *Come bless the Lord*
© David Frost, Pointing © Wm Collins

Come bless the Lord * all you ⏐ servants ·
of the ⏐ Lord:
**you that by night ⏐
stand · in the ⏐ house of · our ⏐ God.**

Lift up your hands toward the holy place
and ⏐ bless the ⏐ Lord:
**may the Lord bless you from Zion *
the ⏐ Lord
   who · made ⏐ heaven · and ⏐ earth.**

**Glory to the Father and ⏐ to the ⏐ Son:
and ⏐ to the ⏐ Holy ⏐ Spirit;
as it was in the be⏐ginning · is ⏐ now:
and shall be for ⏐ ever. ⏐ A⏐men.**

134D

From Psalm 134, Philip Lawson-Johnston
© 1975 Thankyou Music

Come bless the Lord,
all you servants of the Lord
who stand by night
       in the house of the Lord;
lift up your hands to the holy place
and bless the Lord:
   come bless the Lord,
   come bless the Lord!

134L

Psalm 134.1–3
© Editor/Jubilee Hymns

You servants of the Lord,
   who stand in his temple at night:
A **praise the Lord!**

Lift your hands in prayer to the Lord:
A&B **in his sanctuary, praise the Lord!**

May the Lord who made the heaven and
   the earth bless you from Zion:
ALL **Amen!**

**Glory to the Father, and to the Son,
and to the Holy Spirit:
as it was in the beginning, is now,
and shall be for ever. Amen.**

*The congregation may divide at A and B, in
which case the* Gloria *should be used.*

136A

From Psalm 136
© Paul Wigmore/Jubilee Hymns

1 Give thanks to God, the Lord of all
   creation's wonders, great and small,
       whose love endures for ever:
   he gave the splendour of the earth,
   the birth of spring, the winter's death –
       his love endures for ever.

2 And to the joy of human eye
   beyond the earth he set the sky –
       his love endures for ever:
   he blessed the darkness with the light,
   the sun by day, the stars by night –
       his love endures for ever.

3 And from oppression's evil spell
   he led his people Israel –
       his love endures for ever:
   through sea and desert, pain and fear
   their strength was his, for he was near –
       his love endures for ever.

4 Give thanks to God, the God of all,
   for he is good, he hears our call,
     his love endures for ever:
   our God is from eternity,
   he lifts and feeds us, sets us free –
     his love endures for ever.

136B
From Psalm 136
© Michael Perry/Jubilate Hymns

1 Give thanks to God, for he is good,
   give thanks to him, the God of gods,
   give thanks to him, the Lord of lords:
     his love shall last for ever!

2 For God alone works miracles;
   the skies were made at his command,
   he spread the seas upon the earth:
     his love shall last for ever!

3 He made the stars to shine at night,
   he made the sun to shine by day;
   he brought us out from slavery:
     his love shall last for ever!

4 He leads us onward by his grace,
   he saves us from our enemies –
   give thanks to God, for he is good:
     his love shall last for ever!

136C
From Psalm 136, Bob Fraser
© 1985 Ears and Eyes Music Ltd/
Boosey & Hawkes Music Publishers Ltd

1 O give thanks to the Lord for he is good,
   for his love endures for ever;
   O give thanks to the Lord for he is good,
   for his love endures for ever:
   for his steadfast love, his steadfast love,
   his love endures for ever;
   for his steadfast love, his steadfast love,
   his love endures for ever.

2 O give thanks to the God of gods . . .

3 O give thanks to the King of kings . . .

4 O give thanks to the Lord of lords . . .

136L
Psalm 136.1–26
© Editor/Jubilate Hymns

A Give thanks to God, for he is good:
A his love shall last for ever!

B Give thanks to him, the God of gods:
B his love shall last for ever!

C Give thanks to him, the Lord of lords:
C his love shall last for ever!

A For God alone works miracles:
A his love shall last for ever!

B The skies were made at his command:
B his love shall last for ever!

C he spread the seas upon the earth:
C his love shall last for ever!

A He made the stars to shine at night:
A his love shall last for ever!

B He made the sun to shine by day:
B his love shall last for ever!

C He brought us out from slavery:
C his love shall last for ever!

A He leads us onwards by his grace:
A his love shall last for ever!

B He saves us from our enemies:
B his love shall last for ever!

C Give thanks to God, for he is good:
C his love shall last for ever!
ALL **Amen!**

The congregation may divide at A *and* B
saying the whole stanza, OR both minister
and congregation should divide.

137A
From Psalms 137 and 138
© Michael Perry/Jubilate Hymns

1 By rivers of sorrow
       we sat and remembered
   the city of happiness where we belong;
   our harps and our melodies
       hung in the branches,
   and there our tormentors
       demanded a song!

2 O how shall we sing
       in the anguish of exile –
   the songs of the Lord in a far away land?
   Jerusalem, see if I ever forget you
   till death take my voice
       and the skill of my hand!

3 You daughter of Babylon,
       doomed to destruction,
   you people of Edom
       who throw down our walls,
   be warned of the judgement
       on you and your children:
   when blasphemy fails
       and when tyranny falls.

4 And then shall the strings of the harp
       yield their music,
   and then shall the tune of our song
       be restored;
   and then shall the kings of the earth
       see God's purpose,
   the strong, the unquenchable,
       love of the Lord.

137B

From Psalm 137
© Michael Perry/Jubilate Hymns

1 By flowing waters of Babylon
we hung our harps on the willows:
how shall we sing our Jehovah's song
in a foreign land, far away?

2 They who oppress us and mock our grief
tell us to sing and be merry:
how can we worship when spirits fail
in an alien land, far away?

3 If we forget you, Jerusalem,
may we keep silence for ever!
Still we remember our distant home
in another land, far away.

137C

From Psalm 137
© Michael Perry/Jubilate Hymns

1 Babylon
by the rivers of sorrow!
Hang your harps
by the old willow tree.
All our joy is gone,
there's no hope for tomorrow.
We'll never forget you,
O Jerusalem!

2 'Sing', they say,
'all the songs of your city!'
How shall we sing
in an alien land? –
captives brought away
without mercy or pity!
We'll never forget you,
O Jerusalem!

3 Glory be
to the name of the Father:
glory be
for the grace of the Son;
glory be
in the joy of the Spirit:
we look for the mercy
of the Three-in-One!

138A

From Psalm 138
© Michael Perry/Jubilate Hymns

1 I'll praise you, Lord,
with heart content and joyful,
before the world
I'll tell your righteous ways;
I will bow down
towards your holy temple,
and breathe your name
and sing your worthy praise.

2 Beyond the skies
you set your timeless kingdom –
your word shall last,
your throne shall never fall;
the lords of earth
will marvel at your wisdom
and kneel before the mighty Lord of all.

3 Though set on high,
you look upon the lowly –
the proud you know with sorrow
from afar;
in all my trouble you are swift to save me,
and with your arm
restrain the threat of war.

4 For ever
you will keep your face towards us,
your truth, your faithful love –
they will not cease:
then come in power,
fulfil your mighty purpose,
and grant to your creation perfect peace.

138B

From Psalm 138
© International Bible Society

1 I will praise you Lord with all my heart,
before the 'gods' I will sing your praise;
I will bow down to your holy place
and praise your name!

2 I will praise you for your faith and love –
your name and your word
are above all things.
When I called,
you came and answered me
and made me bold and strong.

3 Let the kings of earth praise you, O Lord,
when they hear the words of your mouth;
and let them sing of the ways of the Lord,
for the glory of the Lord is great!

4 Though the Lord is high,
he is near to the low;
but the proud he sees from far away:
and though I walk in the midst of trouble,
you preserve my life!

5 You stretch your hand against my foes,
and you save me by your right hand.
The Lord will see his purpose for me:
your love will last for ever.
Your love will last for ever!

Don't ever leave the works of your hand,
your love will last for ever,
your love will last for ever,
your love will last for ever!

139A

From Psalm 139, Brian Foley
© 1971 Faber Music Ltd

1   There is no moment of my life,
    no place where I may go,
    no action which God does not see,
    no thought he does not know.

2   Before I speak, my words are known,
    and all that I decide.
    To come or go? God knows my choice,
    and makes himself my guide.

3   If I should close my eyes to him,
    he comes to give me sight;
    if I should go where all is dark,
    he makes my darkness light.

4   He knew my days before all days,
    before I came to be;
    he keeps me, loves me, in my ways –
    no lover such as he.

139B

From Psalm 139
© Christopher Idle/Jubilate Hymns

1   Lord all-knowing, you have found me;
    every secret thought and word,
    all my actions, all my longings
    you have seen and you have heard.

2   Lord almighty, you have made me,
    fashioned me to keep your laws;
    your design and your creation,
    every part of me is yours.

3   Lord all-holy, you have judged me
    by a standard true and right;
    all the best I have to offer
    withers in your burning light.

4   Lord all-loving, you have saved me
    in supreme and mighty grace;
    by your Son's triumphant mercy,
    suffering, dying in my place.

5   Lord all-glorious, you receive me
    where your ransomed servants sing;
    you have spoken, rescued, conquered –
    Christ, our prophet, priest, and king!

139C

From Psalm 139
© Colin Avery/Jubilate Hymns

1   O Lord, you know my mind –
    each hidden corner there you find;
    you know each secret thought and deed.
    You are everywhere, all-seeing,
    you have formed my inner being,
    you perceive my every need.

    In your name I rejoice,
    I know you hear my voice,
    I will put my trust in you.
    You are Lord, you are King,
    set above everything:
    I will praise you,
    for all your ways are true –
    Lord, lead me in the way everlasting.

2   If on morning's wings I soar,
    or settle on some distant shore,
    your hand will guide me even there.
    If I seek the depths of night,
    to you the darkness is as light:
    your hand will hold me in your care.
       In your name . . .

3   There is nowhere I can hide –
    you are around, in front, beside me;
    there is nowhere I can flee.
    Though such knowledge is too grand
    for such as me to understand
    you stretched out your right hand to me.
       In your name . . .

4   O Lord, you know my heart
    for you created me, each part:
    examine me and know my ways.
    If I any way offend
    then, Lord, assist me to amend
    that I may offer worthy praise.
       In your name . . .

139D

From Psalm 139, Ian Pitt-Watson
© Ears and Eyes Music Ltd/
Boosey & Hawkes Music Publishers Ltd

1   You are before me, Lord, you are behind,
    and over me
        you have spread out your hand;
    such knowledge is too wonderful for me,
    too high to grasp,
        too great to understand.

2   Then where, Lord, from your presence
        shall I go,
    and from your Spirit
        where, Lord, shall I fly?
    If I ascend to heaven you are there,
    and still are with me if in hell I lie:

3   And if I take my flight into the dawn,
    or if I dwell on ocean's farthest shore,
    your mighty hand will rest upon me still,
    and your right hand
        will guard me evermore.

4 Search me, O God,
       search me and know my ways;
   try me, O God, my mind and spirit try –
   keep me from
       any path that gives you pain,
   and lead me in the everlasting way,
   the everlasting way.

139E
From Psalm 139, Bob Fraser
© 1986 Ears and Eyes Music Ltd/
Boosey & Hawkes Music Publishers Ltd

   Search me, O God,
   and know my heart,
   and deal with any wicked part;
   reveal the darkness and the sin,
   expose the secrets of my soul,
   press to my lips the heated coal,
   and purify my life within.

1 But if I really start to pray
   and from all evil turn away,
   then you are ready to forgive
   and you will make the dry bones live.
       Search me, O God . . .

2 Your cross, a burning bush ahead;
   the ground is holy where I tread:
   and all the guilt and all the shame
   will lift as I look to you again.
       Search me, O God . . .

       . . . and purify my life within.

141
From Psalm 141
© Michael Perry/Jubilate Hymns

1 O Lord, come quickly when I call;
   receive my prayer with favour,
   fair as the evening sacrifice,
   as incense sweet to savour.

   Keep watch upon my mouth, O Lord,
   and guard my lips from evil;
   so turn my heart from wicked ways
   that I may shame the devil.

2 O Lord, I'll seek your discipline –
   but strengthen me to choose it;
   your oil of grace anoints my head –
   my head will not refuse it.

   My eyes are fixed on you, O Lord,
   though dangers yet surround me;
   in life your love will be my rock,
   and death shall not confound me.

142A
From Psalm 142
© Michael Perry/Jubilate Hymns

(CHOIR
   You are my refuge,
   I will praise your name;
   you are good to me, O Lord!)
(ALL
   You are my refuge,
   I will praise your name;
   you are good to me, O Lord!)

1 When I lift up my voice,
   and I cry to the Lord,
   and I pour out my troubles before him:
   I say . . .
       You are my refuge . . .

2 When I see no-one cares,
   and I walk all alone,
   and my spirit grows weary within me:
   I say . . .
       You are my refuge . . .

3 When he comes to my side
   and he answers my prayers,
   and he sets my soul free from its prison:
   I say . . .
       You are my refuge . . .

142B
From Psalm 142
© Michael Perry/Jubilate Hymns

1 When I lift up my voice,
   and I cry to the Lord,
   and I pour out my troubles before him;
   when I see no-one cares,
   and I walk all alone,
   and my spirit grows weary within me,
   then I sing:
       'You are my refuge,
       I will praise your name;
       you are so good to me, O Lord!'
   Then I sing . . .

2 Then he'll come to my side
   and he'll answer my prayers,
   and he'll set my soul free from its prison;
   then the righteous will see
   and they'll gather around
   all because of his goodness towards me,
   then they'll sing:
       'You are our refuge
       we will praise your name;
       you are so good to us, O Lord!'
   Then they'll sing . . .

143A
From Psalm 143
© David Preston/Jubilate Hymns

1 Hear me, O Lord, in my distress,
  give ear to my despairing plea!
  In faithfulness, in righteousness,
  oh, hear my prayer and answer me.

2 I claim no favour as of right;
  you are the God I serve and trust,
  yet judge me not: for in your sight
  no living soul is counted just.

3 My fierce oppressor hunts me down –
  I shrink in darkness, like the dead;
  my spirit fails – all hope is gone,
  my heart is overwhelmed with dread.

4 Days long since vanished I review,
  I see the wonders of your hands,
  and I stretch out my hands to you,
  for you I thirst like desert sands.

5 Lord, answer me without delay!
  I perish if you hide your face;
  in you I trust: let this new day
  bring word of your unfailing grace.

6 For your name's sake,
        Lord, hear my plea:
  your servant's stricken life preserve!
  From all oppression set me free
  to live and love the God I serve.

143B
From Psalm 143
© Barbara Woollett/Jubilate Hymns

1 O Lord, I bring myself to you,
  Christ bears my guilt and shame;
  because you are a faithful God
  I call upon your name:
  when darkness overwhelms my soul
  your promised grace I claim.

2 O Lord, I bring myself to you,
  your mercy to receive;
  each morning keep me in your love
  and all my sins forgive:
  your Holy Spirit fill my soul
  and guide me how to live.

3 O Lord, I bring myself to you
  and give you all my days;
  but need your strength to overcome
  the failure of my ways:
  so, as your light shines in my soul,
  let others learn your praise.

143L
Psalm 143.6–10, and Psalm 51.6–12
© Editor/Jubilate Hymns

O Lord, I spread my hands out to you:
A **I thirst for you like dry ground.**

Teach me to do your will, for you are my
God:
B **let your good Spirit lead me in safety.**

You require sincerity and truth in me:
A **fill my mind with your wisdom.**

Create in me a pure heart, O God:
B **and renew a faithful spirit in me.**

Do not cast me from your presence:
A **or take your Holy Spirit from me.**

Give me again the joy of your salvation:
B **and make me willing to obey.**

**Glory to the Father, and to the Son,
and to the Holy Spirit:
as it was in the beginning, is now,
and shall be for ever. Amen.**

The congregation may divide at A *and* B, *in
which case the Gloria should be used.
Psalms 143 and 51 have been grouped
together to provide for an occasion when the
person and work of the Holy Spirit is being
considered.*

145A
From Psalm 145
© Timothy Dudley-Smith

1 To God our great salvation
      a triumph-song we raise,
  with hymns of adoration
      and everlasting praise.
  That name beyond all naming,
      from age to age adored,
  we lift on high, proclaiming
      the greatness of the Lord.

2 Declare in song and story
      the wonders we confess,
  who hail the King of Glory
      the Lord our Righteousness.
  In loving-kindness caring
      his mercies stand displayed,
  forgiving and forbearing
      to all his hand has made.

3 His kingdom knows no ending,
      enthroned in light sublime,
  his sovereign power extending
      beyond all space and time.
  To us and all things living
      he comes in word and deed,
  forbearing and forgiving,
      to meet us in our need.

4   The King of all creation
     is near to those who call;
    the God of our salvation
     has stooped to save us all.
    Lift high your hearts and voices,
     his praises sound again;
    in God his earth rejoices
     for evermore. Amen!

Glory to the Father and ' to the ' Son:
and ' to the ' Holy ' Spirit;
as it was in the be'ginning · is ' now:
and shall be for ' ever. ' A'men.

145B

From Psalm 145, © David Frost
Pointing © Wm Collins

I will exalt you O ' God my ' king:
I will bless your ' name
for ' ever · and ' ever.
Every ' day · will I ' bless you:
and praise your ' name
for ' ever · and ' ever.

Great is the Lord * and wonderfully '
worthy · to be ' praised:
his greatness is ' past ' searching ' out.
One generation shall praise your '
works · to an'other:
and de'clare your ' mighty ' acts.

Your kingdom is an ever'lasting '
kingdom:
and your dominion en'dures
through ' all · gener'ations.
The Lord upholds all ' those who '
stumble:
and raises up '
those · that are ' bowed ' down.

The eyes of all look to ' you in ' hope:
and you give them their ' food
in ' due ' season;
you open ' wide your ' hand:
and fill all things ' living ·
with your ' bounte·ous ' gift.

The Lord is just in ' all his ' ways:
and ' faithful · in ' all his ' dealings.
The Lord is near to all who ' call up'on
him:
to all who ' call up'on him · in ' truth.

He will fulfil the desire of ' those that ' fear
him:
he will ' hear their ' cry
and ' save them.
The Lord preserves all ' those that ' love
him:
but the wicked '
he will ' utterly · de'stroy.

Second part
My mouth shall speak the ' praises ·
of the ' Lord:
and let all flesh bless his holy ' name
for ' ever · and ' ever.

145C

From Psalm 145
© International Bible Society

1   Worthy, the Lord is worthy,
    and no-one understands
       the greatness of his name.

2   Gracious, so kind and gracious,
    and slow to anger
       and rich, so rich in love:

3   My mouth will speak
       in praise of my Lord:
    let every creature praise his holy name;
     for ever and evermore,
     for ever and evermore;
     for ever and evermore,
     for ever and evermore.

4   Faithful, the Lord is faithful
    to all his promises,
       and loves all he has made.

5   Righteous, in all ways, righteous –
    and he is near
       to all who call on him in truth:
     for ever and evermore . . .

6   Worthy, the Lord is worthy,
    and no-one understands
       the greatness of his name.

145D

From Psalm 145, D Bainbridge
© 1985 Ears and Eyes Music Ltd/
Boosey & Hawkes Music Publishers Ltd

    We come to praise you, Father;
    you are the Lord of lords,
    you are the King of glory, Lord of all.

1   I will proclaim your greatness,
    every day I will praise your name –
    now and for ever people will know
     of your glory and majesty:
    your creatures, Lord, will praise you,
     so that people might know
    that your rule is eternal
    and you will be king for ever.
     We come to praise you, . . .

2 The Lord is faithful,
  he will save those who fall;
  all living things can look to him
    for he will satisfy,
  for he is righteous,
  he is near those who call:
  honour him, sing praises,
  proclaim with me his greatness.
    We come to praise you, Father;
    you are the Lord of lords,
    you are the King of glory, Lord of all.

3 Praise the Lord for times and seasons,
  cloud and sunshine, wind and rain;
  spring to melt the snows of winter
  till the waters flow again;
  grass upon the mountain pastures,
  golden valleys thick with grain.

4 Fill your hearts with joy and gladness,
  peace and plenty crown your days;
  love his laws, declare his judgements,
  walk in all his words and ways;
  he the Lord and we his children –
  praise the Lord, all people, praise!

146 From Psalm 146
© Timothy Dudley-Smith

1 Praise the God of our salvation,
  all life long your voices raise!
  Stir your hearts to adoration,
  set your souls to sing his praise!

2 Turn to him, his help entreating;
  only in his mercy trust:
  human pomp and power are fleeting;
  mortal flesh is born for dust.

3 Thankful hearts his praise have sounded
  down the ages long gone by:
  happy they whose hopes are founded
  in the God of earth and sky!

4 Faithful Lord of all things living –
  by his bounty all are blessed,
  bread to hungry bodies giving,
  justice to the long-oppressed.

5 For the strength of our salvation,
  light and life and length of days,
  praise the King of all creation,
  set your souls to sing his praise!

147A From Psalm 147
© Timothy Dudley-Smith

1 Fill your hearts with joy and gladness,
  sing and praise your God and mine!
  Great the Lord in love and wisdom,
  might and majesty divine!
  He who framed the starry heavens
  knows and names them as they shine.

2 Praise the Lord, his people, praise him!
  Wounded souls his comfort know.
  Those who fear him find his mercies,
  peace for pain and joy for woe;
  humble hearts are high exalted,
  human pride and power laid low.

147B From Psalm 147
© Barbara Woollett/Jubilate Hymns

1 O let the Church rejoice
  in God our saviour's grace,
  for it is good to voice
  his all-deserving praise:
    Sing alleluia, praise the Lord –
    he builds his church
    and spreads his word!

2 Our God commands the storm
  and sends the warming breeze;
  he can within us form
  a life of joy and peace.
    Sing alleluia . . .

3 He makes the meadow flower,
  the clouds, the wind and rain;
  the humble, by his power
  he'll lovingly sustain.
    Sing alleluia . . .

4 The broken-hearted sigh –
  he bears their guilt and shame;
  like numbered stars on high
  he knows them all by name.
    Sing alleluia . . .

5 Hope in the Lord above –
  he will provide our needs;
  trust his unfailing love
  praise all his gracious deeds!
    Sing alleluia . . .

147C From Psalm 147, Dale Garratt
© 1980 Scripture in Song/Thankyou Music

  Great is the Lord
  and mighty in power;
  his understanding has no limit.
The Lord delights in those who fear him,
who put their hope in his unfailing love.
He strengthens the bars of your gates,
he grants you peace in your borders,
he reveals his word to his people –
he has done this for no other nation.

Great is the Lord
and mighty in power;
his understanding has no limit.
Extol the Lord, O Jerusalem;
praise your God, O people of Zion.

147D
From Psalm 147
© International Bible Society

1 How good it is to sing
    praise to our God –
    the right and pleasant thing
    to praise his name!

2 The Lord is building up
    Jerusalem;
    he gathers all the lost
    of Israel.

3 He is healing the broken-hearted,
    he is binding all their wounds;
    he determines the stars in the heavens
    and he calls them each by name.

4 Great is the Lord in power;
    all things he knows.
    He casts the wicked down
    but lifts the low!

147E
From Psalm 147, Rich Cook
© 1987 Integrity's Hosanna! Music

The Lord is building Jerusalem,
the Lord is building Jerusalem,
gathering together the outcasts of Israel,
healing broken hearts,
binding up their wounds.
The Lord is building,
the Lord is building up Jerusalem.

147L
Psalm 147.1–20
© Editor/Jubilate Hymns

O praise the Lord, sing out to God:
such praise is right and good.

The Lord restores Jerusalem:
A **he brings the exiles home.**

He heals all those with broken hearts:
B **he bandages their wounds.**

He counts the number of the stars:
C **he calls them each by name.**

How great and mighty is the Lord:
A **immeasurably wise!**

He raises up the humble ones:
B **and brings the mighty down.**

Sing hymns of triumph to his name:
C **make music to our God!**

He spreads the clouds across the sky:
A **he showers the earth with rain.**

He sends the animals their food:
B **he feeds the hungry birds.**

His true delight is not the strong:
C **but those who trust his love.**

Extol the Lord, Jerusalem:
A **let Zion worship God!**

For God shall keep your people safe:
B **and bring your harvest home.**

He gives commandment to the earth:
C **his will is quickly done.**

He spreads like wool the falling snow:
A **how cold the frosty air!**

He sends the wind, the warming rain:
B **and melts the ice away.**

His laws he gives to Israel:
C **and Judah hears his word.**

He does not favour other lands:
ALL **so, praise the Lord. Amen!**

The congregation may divide at A, B and C.

148A
From Psalm 148
© Timothy Dudley-Smith

1 Praise the Lord of heaven,
    praise him in the height;
    praise him, all his angels,
    praise him, hosts of light.
    Sun and moon together,
    shining stars aflame,
    planets in their courses,
    magnify his name!

2 Earth and ocean praise him;
    mountains, hills and trees;
    fire and hail and tempest,
    wind and storm and seas.
    Praise him, fields and forests,
    birds on flashing wings,
    praise him, beasts and cattle,
    all created things.

3 Now by prince and people
    let his praise be told;
    praise him, men and maidens,
    praise him, young and old.
    He, the Lord of glory!
    We, his praise proclaim!
    High above all heavens
    magnify his name!

148B
From Psalm 148
© Michael Perry/Jubilee Hymns

1 Praise him, praise him, praise him,
      powers and dominations!
Praise his name in glorious light,
      you creatures of the day!
Moon and stars, ring praises
      through the constellations:
Lord God, whose word
      shall never pass away!

2 Praise him, praise him, praise him,
      ocean depths and waters!
Elements of earth and heaven,
      your several praises blend!
Birds and beasts and cattle,
      Adam's sons and daughters,
worship the king
      whose reign shall never end!

3 Praise him, praise him, praise him,
      saints of God who fear him!
To the highest name of all,
      concerted anthems raise,
all you seed of Israel,
      holy people near him
whom he exalts
      and crowns with endless praise!

4 Praise God, all lands and seas,
      all living things,
all trees and plants
      that he has made to grow;
all birds and beasts, praise,
      each in your own way,
his greatness,
      which all things created show.

5 Praise God, all men and women,
      young and old –
creation's highest praise is yours to sing;
to honour God,
      to praise with every praise
his Being, everywhere, in everything.

148C
From Psalm 148, Brian Foley
© 1971 Faber Music Ltd

1 All things that are,
      praise God by what they are –
their being speaks to us of God who is;
so we may call on them
      to praise his name,
to give with us the honour that is his.

2 Praise God, all angels made by him to be
for ever in the service of his throne;
shine, sun and moon,
      all stars whose light we see,
and by your shining
      make his great light known.

3 Praise God, all earthly things
      that he has made,
come, cold of winter, heat of summer sun;
come, spring and autumn,
      change and change again,
show in your changing
      how his will is done.

148D
From Psalm 148
Bill Batstone and Tom Howard
© 1982 Maranatha! Music/Word Music (UK)

Praise the Lord,
      praise the Lord from the heavens;
all the angels sing, 'Praise the Lord!'
Praise the Lord –
from the heights of creation
they shall praise the name of the Lord.

1 He commanded them
and the heavens were made;
he established them,
and they won't pass away:
the sun and moon
praise the Lord with their light;
all the stars up above,
they keep shining through the night.
      Praise the Lord . . .

2 And on the earth
let all nature agree –
from the mountain-tops
to the depths of the sea:
the winds and rain
and the fiery light,
all the beasts of the field,
all the birds in their flight.
      Praise the Lord . . .

3 All the people
who inhabit the world,
from the ruling kings
to the boys and the girls;
the young and old
join in praise to his name:
God alone is supreme
let creation proclaim!
      Praise the Lord . . .

148E
From Psalm 148
© Colin Avery/Jubilate Hymns

1 Praise the Lord, dark and light,
day and night, praise him (praise him)!
Praise the Lord, space and sky,
land and sea, praise him (praise him)!
Praise the Lord, sun and moon;
stars and planets, praise him (praise him);
all creation, join to sing his glory!
   I will praise the Lord
   with a song of thanks,
   I will praise the Lord
   with a song of joy;
   I will praise his name for ever,
   praise his glorious name for ever!
   I will praise the Lord for evermore.

2 Praise the Lord, fruit and seeds,
plants and trees, praise him (praise him)!
Praise the Lord, fish and birds,
beasts and cattle, praise him (praise him)!
Praise the Lord, living creatures,
all that breathes, praise him (praise him);
all creation, join to sing his glory!
   I will praise . . .

3 Praise the Lord, young and old,
men and women, praise him (praise him)!
Praise the Lord, rulers, judges,
kings and princes, praise him
      (praise him)!
Praise the Lord, heavenly hosts,
all his angels, praise him (praise him);
all creation, join to sing his glory!
   I will praise . . .

4 Praise the Lord, grass and rivers,
hills and mountains, praise him
      (praise him)!
Praise the Lord, fire and hail,
wind and rain, praise him (praise him)!
Praise the Lord, all the earth,
all of heaven, praise him (praise him);
all creation, join to sing his glory!
   I will praise . . .

148F
From Psalm 148
© Timothy Dudley-Smith

1 Praise the Lord of heaven,
praise him in the height;
praise him, all his angels,
praise him, hosts of light.
Sun and moon together,
shining stars aflame,
planets in their courses,
magnify his name
(O magnify his name)!

2 Earth and ocean, praise him;
mountains, hills and trees,
fire and hail and tempest,
wind and storm and seas.
Praise him, fields and forests,
birds on flashing wings,
praise him, beasts and cattle,
all created things
(yes, all created things)!

3 Now by prince and people
let his praise be told;
praise him, men and maidens,
praise him, young and old.
He, the Lord of glory!
We, his praise proclaim!
High above all heavens
magnify his name
(O magnify his name)!

148G
From Psalm 148
© Richard Bewes/Jubilate Hymns

1 Praise the Lord our God,
   praise the Lord;
praise him from the heights,
   praise the Lord;
praise him, angel throngs,
   praise the Lord –
praise God, all his host!

2 Praise him, sun and moon,
   all the stars;
praise him, sky and clouds,
   rain and snow;
let them praise his name,
   works of God –
all creatures, praise the Lord!

3 Praise him, wind and storm,
   mountains steep;
praise him, fruitful trees,
   cedars tall;
beasts and cattle herds,
   birds that fly –
all creatures, praise the Lord!

4 Kings of earth, give praise,
   rulers all;
all young men and girls,
   praise the Lord;
old men, children small,
   praise the Lord –
all people, praise the Lord!

148L
Psalm 148.1–14
© Editor/Jubilate Hymns

Praise the Lord!

Praise the Lord from the heavens:
praise him in the heights above.

Praise him, all his angels:
A **praise him, all his heavenly host.**

Praise him, sun and moon:
B **praise him, all you shining stars.**

Let them praise the name of the Lord:
ALL **Praise the Lord!**

Praise the Lord from the earth:
A **praise him, great sea creatures.**

Praise him, storms and clouds:
B **praise him, mountains and hills.**

Praise him, fields and woods:
A **praise him, animals and birds.**

Praise him, rulers and nations:
B **praise him, old and young.**

Let them praise the name of the Lord:
ALL **Praise the Lord! Amen.**

The congregation may divide at A *and* B.

149A
From Psalms 149 and 150
© Michael Perry/Jubilate Hymns

1 Bring to the Lord a glad new song,
children of grace extol your king;
your love and praise to God belong –
to instruments of music, sing!
Let those be warned
who spurn God's name,
let rulers all obey God's word,
for justice shall bring tyrants shame –
let every creature praise the Lord!

2 Sing praise within these hallowed walls,
worship beneath the dome of heaven;
by cymbals' sounds and trumpets' calls
let praises fit for God be given:
with strings and brass and wind rejoice –
then, join our song in full accord
all living things with breath and voice;
let every creature praise the Lord!

149B
From Psalm 149, J E Seddon (1915–1983)
© Mrs M Seddon/Jubilate Hymns

Sing a new song – Alleluia!
Sing aloud to God the king;
let the saints of God adore him,
let their joyful praises ring!

1 Let instruments and voices
make music to the Lord;
be glad, O ransomed people,
rejoice with one accord!
The Lord accepts the service
of those who love his name;
he leads them on in triumph
his greatness to proclaim.
Sing a new song . . .

2 They wield the sword of justice,
for God their hands are strong;
they challenge kings and nations,
and fight all forms of wrong:
they work for truth and goodness,
the noble and the right;
and this will be their glory –
to triumph in the fight.
Sing a new song . . .

149L
Psalm 149.1–9
© Editor/Jubilate Hymns

Praise the Lord:
praise the Lord!

Sing a new song to the Lord:
A **let the people shout his name!**

Praise your maker, Israel:
A **hail your king, Jerusalem.**

Sing and dance to honour him:
A **praise him
with the strings and drums.**

God takes pleasure in his saints::
B **crowns the meek with victory.**

Rise, you saints, in triumph now:
A **sing the joyful night away!**

Shout aloud and praise your God!
B **Hold aloft the two-edged sword!**

Let the judgement now begin:
A **kings shall fall and tyrants die.**

Through his people, by his word:
B **God shall have the victory!**

Praise the Lord:
ALL **praise the Lord!**

**Glory to the Father, and to the Son,
and to the Holy Spirit:
as it was in the beginning, is now,
and shall be for ever, Amen.**

*The congregation – and ministers – may
divide at* A *and* B.

150A

From Psalm 150, Fred Kaan
© Stainer & Bell Ltd

1 Praise the Lord with joyful cry;
   let the mood of praise run high.
   Praise him who with mighty deeds
   human greatness far exceeds:
     Alleluia!

2 Praise him with the sound that swings,
   with percussion, brass and strings.
   Let the world at every chance
   praise him with a song and dance:
     Alleluia!

3 Praise with life and voice the Lord,
   him who speaks in deed and word,
   who to life the world ordained –
   let our praise be unrestrained:
     Alleluia!

150B

Psalm 150
© David Frost

CHOIR
Let everything that has breath praise the
Lord:
ALL
Let everything that has breath
praise the Lord!

CHOIR
O praise God in his sanctuary, praise him
in the firmament of his power; praise him
for his mighty acts, praise him according
to his abundant goodness:
ALL
Let everything that has breath
praise the Lord!

CHOIR
Praise him in the blast of the ram's horn,
praise him on the lute and harp, praise
him with the timbrels and dances, praise
him on the strings and pipe:
ALL
Let everything that has breath
praise the Lord!

CHOIR
Praise him on the high-sounding cymbals,
praise him on the loud cymbals; let
everything that has breath praise the
Lord:
ALL
Let everything that has breath
praise the Lord!

CHOIR
Praise the Lord!

150C

Psalm 150, © David Frost
Pointing © Wm Collins

1 O praise ' God · in his ' sanctuary:
praise him
   in the ' firma·ment ' of his ' power.

2 Praise him for his ' mighty ' acts:
praise him according to ' his
   a'bundant ' goodness.

3 Praise him in the ' blast · of the ' ram's
horn:
praise him up'on the ' lute and ' harp.

4 Praise him with the ' timbrel · and '
dances:
praise him
   up'on the ' strings and ' pipe.

5 Praise him on the ' high · sounding '
cymbals:
praise him up'on the ' loud ' cymbals.

6 Let everything that has breath ' praise the
' Lord:
O ' praise'— the ' Lord.

Glory to the Father and ' to the ' Son:
and ' to the ' Holy ' Spirit;
as it was in the be'ginning · is ' now:
and shall be for ' ever. ' A'men.

150D

From Psalm 150
© Stephen Horsfall/Jubilate Hymns

1 Praise God within his holy place,
   come, praise the Lord;
  praise God for all his acts of grace,
   come, praise the Lord.
  Praise God for all his acts of power,
   come, praise the Lord;
  praise him with trumpet, harp and lyre,
   come, praise the Lord!

2 Praise him with tambourine and dance,
   come, praise the Lord;
  with strings and woodwind instruments,
   come, praise the Lord!
  Let cymbals' crash proclaim his love,
   come, praise the Lord;
  praise him because you live and move,
   come, praise the Lord!

150E

From Psalm 150
Author unknown

1 Praise him in his sanctuary,
   praise him in the skies above,
   praise him
         for the acts of power that he does;
   praise him for surpassing greatness,
   with the trumpet, harp and lyre,
   with the tambourine and dancing
         praise him now!
     Come and praise him,
     for the Lord is good,
     and his mercy's everlasting;
     come and praise him,
     for the Lord is good,
     and his mercy's everlasting!

2 Praise him with the clashing cymbals –
   let them hear it far and near:
   with the strings and flute
         we'll praise the Lord our God,
   who with majesty is reigning.
   He has power over all:
   give him glory,
         and be thankful for his love!
     Come and praise him . . .

150F

From Psalm 150, Bob Fraser
© 1985 Ears and Eyes Music Ltd/
Boosey & Hawkes Music Publishers Ltd

   Praise the Lord,
   sing him a new song –
   Zion, awake and sing;
   praise the Lord,
   sing him a new song –
   Zion, rejoice in your King!

1 Praise the Lord
         with every breath that you breathe;
   praise the Lord, rejoice
         all you that believe.
     Praise the Lord . . .

2 Praise the Lord for all his mighty power;
   praise the Lord every day and hour.
     Praise the Lord . . .

3 Praise the Lord,
         with tambourine and string;
   praise the Lord, let every cymbal ring.
     Praise the Lord . . .

150G

From Psalm 150, John Kennett
© 1981 Thankyou Music

   Praise him on the trumpet,
   the psaltery and harp,
   praise him on the timbrel
   and the dance,
   praise him with stringed instruments too;

praise him on the loud cymbals,
praise him on the loud cymbals –
let everything that has breath
praise the Lord!
Alleluia, praise the Lord,
alleluia, praise the Lord –
let everything that has breath
praise the Lord!
Alleluia . . .

150L

Psalm 150.1–6
© Editor/Jubilate Hymns

Praise the Lord!

Praise God in his sanctuary:
praise his strength beyond the skies!

Praise him for his acts of power:
A **praise him
     for his surpassing greatness.**

Praise him with the sounding of the
trumpet:
B **praise him with the harp and lyre.**

Praise him with the tambourine and
dancing:
A **praise him with the strings and flute.**

Praise him with the clash of cymbals:
B **praise hm with resounding cymbals.**

Let everything that has breath praise the
Lord:
ALL **Praise the Lord! Amen.**

   **Glory to the Father, and to the Son,
   and to the Holy Spirit:
   as it was in the beginning, is now,
   and shall be for ever. Amen.**

The congregation may divide at A *and* B.

151

From Psalms 95 and 96, *Venite*
© David Frost, Pointing © Wm Collins

1 O come let us sing | out · to the | Lord:
   **let us shout in triumph
   to the | rock of | our sal'vation.**
2 Let us come before his | face with |
   thanksgiving:
   **and cry | out to · him | joyfully ·
   in | psalms.**

3 For the Lord is a | great | God:
   and a great | king a·bove | all | gods.
4 In his hand are the | depths · of the | earth:
   **and the peaks of the | mountains ·
   are | his | also.**

Second part

5 The sea is his and ' he ' made it:
    his hands ' moulded ' dry ' land.

6 Come let us worship and ' bow ' down:
    and kneel be'fore the ' Lord
      our ' maker.

7 For he is the ' Lord our ' God:
    we are his ' people ·
    and the ' sheep of · his ' pasture.

8 If only you would hear his ' voice to'day:
    for he ' comes to ' judge the ' earth.

9 He shall judge the ' world with '
    righteousness:
    and the ' peoples ' with his ' truth.

    Glory to the Father and ' to the ' Son:
    and ' to the ' Holy ' Spirit;
    as it was in the be'ginning · is ' now:
    and shall be for ' ever. ' A'men.

152A
From 1 Corinthians 5 and 15 and Romans 6,
The Easter Anthems
© David Mowbray/Jubilate Hymns

1 Now lives the Lamb of God,
    our Passover, the Christ,
    who once with nails and wood
    for us was sacrificed:
      Come, keep the feast, the anthem sing
      that Christ indeed is Lord and king!

2 Now risen from the dead
    Christ never dies again;
    in us, with Christ as head,
    sin nevermore shall reign:
      Come, keep the feast . . .

3 In Adam all must die,
    forlorn and unforgiven;
    in Christ we come alive,
    the second Man from heaven.
      Come, keep the feast . . .

4 Give praise to God alone
    who life from death can bring;
    whose mighty power can turn
    our winter into spring:
      Come, keep the feast . . .

152B
From 1 Corinthians 5 and 15 and Romans 6,
The Easter Anthems ASB © 1980 The Central
Board of Finance of the Church of England

1 Christ our passover has been '
    sacri·ficed ' for us:
    so let us ' cele'brate the ' feast,
2 not with the old leaven of cor'ruption ·
    and ' wickedness:
    but with the unleavened ' bread
      of · sin'cerity · and ' truth.

3 Christ once raised from the dead ' dies
    no ' more:
    death has no ' more do'minion '
      over him.

4 In dying he died to sin ' once for ' all:
    in ' living · he ' lives to ' God.

5 See yourselves therefore as ' dead to ' sin:
    and alive to God
    in ' Jesus ' Christ our ' Lord.

6 Christ has been ' raised · from the ' dead:
    the ' firstfruits · of ' those who ' sleep.

7 For as by ' man came ' death:
    by man has come also
    the resur'rection ' of the ' dead;

8 for as in ' Adam · all ' die:
    even so
    in Christ shall ' all be ' made a'live.

    Glory to the Father and ' to the ' Son:
    and ' to the ' Holy ' Spirit;
    as it was in the be'ginning · is ' now:
    and shall be for ' ever. ' A'men.

153A
From Luke 1,
Song of Zechariah/Benedictus
© Michael Perry/Jubilate Hymns

1 O bless the God of Israel,
      who comes to set us free,
    who visits and redeems us
      and grants us liberty.
    The prophets spoke of mercy,
      of rescue and release;
    God shall fulfil the promise
      to bring our people peace.

2 Now from the house of David
      a child of grace is given;
    a Saviour comes among us
      to raise us up to heaven.
    Before him goes the herald,
      forerunner in the way,
    the prophet of salvation,
      the messenger of Day.

3 Where once were fear and darkness
      the sun begins to rise –
    the dawning of forgiveness
      upon the sinner's eyes,
    to guide the feet of pilgrims
      along the paths of peace:
    O bless our God and Saviour,
      with songs that never cease!

153B

From Luke 1,
Song of Zechariah/Benedictus
© Michael Hewlett

1 O praise our great and faithful God,
the God our parents knew,
for in his Name the prophets spoke,
and we have found them true.

2 The oath he swore to save us all
he kept, and it was done:
protection, pardon, peace and hope,
we have them in his Son.

3 O children's children, you in turn
shall go before his face,
to give the knowledge of his love
and to prepare his ways.

4 Tell them the Dayspring from on high
has dawned for our release:
benighted, lost, in fear of death,
the world can know our peace.

5 To Father, Son and Spirit, praise!
To God whom we adore
be worship, glory, power and love,
both now and evermore!

153C

From Luke 1, *Song of Zechariah/Benedictus*
© International Consultation on English Texts

1 Blessed be the Lord the ' God of ' Israel:
**for he has come to his ' people ·
and ' set them ' free.**
2 He has raised up for us a ' mighty '
saviour:
**born of the ' house ·
of his ' servant ' David.**
3 Through his holy prophets he '
promised · of ' old:
**that he would save us
from our enemies ***
from the ' hands of ' all that ' hate us.
4 He promised to show ' mercy · to our '
fathers:
**and to re'member ·
his ' holy ' covenant.**
5 This was the oath he swore to our '
father ' Abraham:
**to set us ' free · from the ' hands
of · our ' enemies,**
6 free to worship him with'out ' fear:
**holy and righteous in his sight '
all the ' days of · our ' life.**
7 You my child shall be called the prophet
of the ' Most ' High:
**for you will go before the ' Lord ·
to pre'pare his ' way,**

8 to give his people knowledge ' of
sal'vation:
by the for'giveness · of ' all their ' sins.
9 In the tender compassion ' of our ' God:
**the dawn from on ' high
shall ' break up'on us,**
10 to shine on those who dwell in darkness
and the ' shadow · of ' death:
**and to guide our feet '
into · the ' way of ' peace.**

**Glory to the Father and ' to the ' Son:
and ' to the ' Holy ' Spirit;
as it was in the be'ginning · is ' now:
and shall be for ' ever. ' A'men.**

153D

From Luke 1,
Song of Zechariah/Benedictus
© David Mowbray/Jubilate Hymns

1 Blessed be the God of Israel
who sets his people free;
the mighty saviour has appeared
to bring us liberty.

2 This news fulfils God's word which came
to prophets long before:
the promise made to Abraham,
the solemn oath God swore.

3 Among us walks the Lord Most High!
How favoured is the child
who bids God's people turn from sin,
and so be reconciled!

4 Earth's shadows shall be swept away
and darkness shall decrease,
and God's compassion brightly shine
to guide our feet in peace.

153E

From Luke 1,
Song of Zechariah/Benedictus
© David Mowbray/Jubilate Hymns

1 O praise the Lord,
the mighty god of Israel,
redeemer of his people
he has come;
he raises up
the dynasty of David
as promised by his prophets
long ago.

2 Salvation from the hands
of those who hate us!
His covenant with Abraham
fulfilled!
He rescues us that, fearless,
we might serve him
in honour and in goodness
all our days.

3 And you will be the
 prophet of the Highest,
to go before him
 and prepare his way;
to give his people
 knowledge of salvation,
the blessing of forgiveness
 for their sins.

4 The Lord our God has shown
 his tender mercy,
his shining sun will come to us
 from heaven
to dawn on those who live
 in death's dark shadow,
and guide our footsteps
 in the path of peace.

154A

From *A Song of Creation/Benedicite*
© Judy Davies/Jubilate Hymns

1 Bless the Lord, created things,
highest heavens, angel host;
bless the Father, Spirit, Son:
 worship, all creation.

2 Sun and moon and stars of heaven,
showery waters, rain and dew,
stormy gale and fiery heat:
 worship, all creation.

3 Scorching wind and bitter cold,
icy blizzard, morning mist,
light and darkness, nights and days:
 worship, all creation.

4 Frosty air and falling snow,
clouds and lightnings, dales and hills,
all that grows upon the earth:
 worship, all creation.

5 Springs and rivers, ocean deeps,
whales and fishes of the sea,
prowling beasts and soaring birds:
 worship, all creation.

6 All on earth who serve our God,
priests and people of the Lord,
upright, holy, humble hearts:
 worship, all creation.

154B

From *A Song of Creation/Benedicite*
© Michael Perry/Jubilate Hymns

Angels, praise him,
heavens, praise him,
waters, praise him,
 Alleluia!
creatures of the Lord,
all praise him
 for evermore:

2 Sun, praise him,
moon, praise him,
stars, praise him,
 Alleluia!
showers, praise him,
dews, praise him
 for evermore:

WOMEN
3 Wind, praise him,
fire, praise him,
heat, praise him,
 Alleluia!
winter, praise him,
summer, praise him
 for evermore:

MEN
4 Nights, praise him,
days, praise him,
light, praise him,
 Alleluia!
lightnings, praise him,
clouds, praise him
 for evermore:

WOMEN
5 Earth, praise him,
mountains, praise him,
hills, praise him,
 Alleluia!
green things, praise him,
wells, praise him
 for evermore:

MEN
6 Seas, praise him,
rivers, praise him,
fish, praise him,
 Alleluia!
birds, praise him,
beasts, praise him
 for evermore:

7 Nations, praise him,
churches, praise him,
saints, praise him,
 Alleluia!
all his people,
join to praise him
 for evermore!

154C

From *A Song of Creation/Benedicite*
ASB © 1980 The Central Board
of Finance of the Church of England

1 Bless the Lord all cre'ated ' things:
**sing his ' praise ·
and ex'alt him · for ' ever.**
2 Bless the ' Lord you ' heavens:
**sing his ' praise ·
and ex'alt him · for ' ever.**

3 Bless the Lord you ¦ angels · of the ¦ Lord:
  bless the ¦ Lord all ¦ you his ¦ hosts;
4 bless the Lord all ¦ men · on the ¦ earth:
  sing his ¦ praise ·
  and ex¦alt him · for ¦ ever.

5 O people of God ¦ bless the ¦ Lord:
  bless the ¦ Lord
    you ¦ priests · of the ¦ Lord;
6 bless the Lord you ¦ servants · of the ¦
  Lord:
  sing his ¦ praise ·
  and ex¦alt him · for ¦ ever.

7 Bless the Lord all men of ¦ upright ¦ spirit:
  bless the Lord
  you that are ¦ holy ·
    and ¦ humble · in ¦ heart.
  Bless the Father the Son
    and the ¦ Holy ¦ Spirit:
  sing his ¦ praise ·
  and ex¦alt him · for ¦ ever.

155A
From *Great and wonderful*
© Christopher Idle/Jubilate Hymns

1 Great and wonderful your deeds,
  God from whom all power proceeds;
  true and right are all your ways –
  who shall not give thanks and praise?
    To your name be glory!

2 King of nations, take your crown!
  Every race shall soon bow down.
  Holy God and Lord alone,
  justice in your deeds is shown;
    all have seen your glory.

3 To the one almighty God,
  to the Lamb who shed his blood,
  to the Spirit now be given
  by the hosts of earth and heaven
    love and praise and glory!

155B
From *Great and wonderful*
© David Mowbray/Jubilate Hymns

1 Wonderful your deeds, Lord,
  just and true your ways;
  you are God almighty,
  king beyond all praise.

2 Holy is your name, Lord:
  fill our hearts with awe!
  Who shall not revere you
  now and evermore?

3 Nations bow in worship,
  kneeling at your throne;
  faithful are your dealings,
  all your judgements known.

4 Praise to God the Father,
  praise to Christ the Lamb,
  and to God the Spirit
  ever and amen!

155C
Great and wonderful
© Joint Liturgical Group

1 Great and wonderful are your deeds
  Lord ¦ God · the Al¦mighty:
  just and true are your ¦ ways
  O ¦ King · of the ¦ nations.

2 Who shall not revere and praise your ¦
  name O ¦ Lord?
  for ¦ you a¦lone are ¦ holy.

3 All nations shall come and worship ¦ in
  your ¦ presence:
  for your just ¦ dealings ·
    have ¦ been re¦vealed.

  To him who sits on the throne ¦
  and · to the ¦ Lamb:
  be praise and honour
  glory and might *
  for ever and ¦ ever. ¦ A¦men.

155D
From *Great and Wonderful*
© Joint Liturgical Group

  Great and wonderful are your deeds,
  Lord God the almighty;
  just and true are your ways,
  O King of the nations!

1 Who shall not revere and praise
    your name, O Lord?
  for you alone are holy.
    Great and wonderful . . .

2 All nations shall come and worship
    in your presence,
  for your just dealings
    have been revealed.
    Great and wonderful . . .

  To him who sits on the throne
    and to the Lamb
  be praise and honour, glory and might
  for ever and ever. Amen, amen, amen.

156A
From *Te Deum*
© Timothy Dudley-Smith

1 God of gods, we sound his praises,
  highest heaven its homage brings;
  earth and all creation raises
  glory to the King of kings:
    holy, holy, holy, name him,
    Lord of all his hosts proclaim him;
  to the everlasting Father
  every tongue in triumph sings.

2 Christians in their hearts enthrone him,
tell his praises wide abroad;
prophets, priests, apostles own him
martyrs' crown and saints' reward.
   Three-in-One his glory sharing,
   earth and heaven his praise declaring,
praise the high majestic Father,
praise the everlasting Lord!

3 Hail the Christ, the King of glory,
he whose praise the angels cry;
born to share our human story,
love and labour, grieve and die:
   by his cross his work completed,
   sinners ransomed, death defeated;
in the glory of the Father
Christ ascended reigns on high.

4 Lord, we look for your returning;
teach us so to walk your ways,
hearts and minds your will discerning,
lives alight with joy and praise:
   in your love and care enfold us,
   by your constancy uphold us;
may your mercy, Lord and Father,
keep us now and all our days!

156B

From *Te Deum*
© Christopher Idle/Jubilate Hymns

1 God, we praise you! God, we bless you!
God, we name you sovereign Lord!
Mighty King whom angels worship,
Father, by your church adored:
all creation shows your glory,
heaven and earth draw near your throne
singing 'Holy, holy, holy,
Lord of hosts, and God alone!'

2 True apostles, faithful prophets,
saints who set their world ablaze,
martyrs, once unknown, unheeded,
join one growing song of praise,
while your church on earth confesses
one majestic Trinity:
Father, Son, and Holy Spirit,
God, our hope eternally.

3 Jesus Christ, the king of glory,
everlasting Son of God,
humble was your virgin mother,
hard the lonely path you trod:
by your cross is sin defeated,
hell confronted face to face,
heaven opened to believers,
sinners justified by grace.

4 Christ, at God's right hand victorious,
you will judge the world you made;
Lord, in mercy help your servants
for whose freedom you have paid:
raise us up from dust to glory,
guard us from all sin today;
King enthroned above all praises,
save your people, God, we pray.

156C

Te Deum, © International
Consultation on English Texts

1 You are ˈ God · and we ˈ praise you:
you are the ˈ Lord
and ˈ we acˈclaim you;
2 you are the eˈternal ˈ Father:
all creˈation ˈ worships ˈ you.

3 To you all angels *
all the ˈ powers of ˈ heaven:
cherubim and seraphim ˈ
sing in ˈ endless ˈ praise,
4 Holy holy holy Lord *
God of ˈ power and ˈ might:
heaven and ˈ earth
are ˈ full of · your ˈ glory.

5 The glorious company of aˈpostles ˈ
praise you:
the noble fellowship of prophets
  praise you *
the white-robed ˈ army · of ˈ martyrs ˈ
  praise you.
6 Throughout the world the holy ˈ Church
acˈclaims you:
Father of ˈ majesˈty unˈbounded;

Second part
7 your true and only Son *
worthy of ˈ all ˈ worship:
and the Holy ˈ Spirit ˈ
  advocate · and ˈ guide.

8 You Christ are the ˈ King of ˈ glory:
the eˈternal ˈ Son · of the ˈ Father.
9 When you became man to ˈ set us ˈ free:
you did not abˈhor the ˈ Virgin's ˈ womb.

10 You overcame the ˈ sting of ˈ death:
and opened the kingdom of ˈ heaven ·
  to ˈ all beˈlievers.
11 You are seated at God's right ˈ hand in ˈ
glory:
we believe that you will ˈ come
and ˈ be our ˈ judge.

12 Come then Lord and ˈ help your ˈ
people:
bought with the ˈ price
  of ˈ your own ˈ blood;
13 and bring us ˈ with your ˈ saints:
to ˈ glory ˈ everˈlasting.

14 Save your people Lord and ' bless ·
your in'heritance:
**govern and up'hold them '
now and ' always.**
15 Day by ' day we ' bless you:
we ' praise your ' name for ' ever.

16 Keep us today Lord from ' all ' sin:
**have mercy ' on us ' Lord
have ' mercy.**
17 Lord show us your ' love and ' mercy:
for we ' put our ' trust in ' you.

Second part
18 In you Lord ' is our ' hope:
let us not be con'founded ' at the ' last.

156D
From *Te Deum*
© David Mowbray/Jubilate Hymns

1 Great is the Lord we now acclaim –
God everlasting is his name:
let heaven and earth with music ring,
and 'Holy, holy, holy' sing!

2 Let prophets and apostles join
with martyrs in triumphant line
to echo the angelic cry
and celebrate God's mystery.

3 We praise God's true and only Son,
for ever with the Father one;
we praise the Spirit at their side,
the Church's advocate and guide.

4 When once the time had fully come
Christ did not scorn the Virgin's womb;
our Lord the sting of death defied
and flung the gate of heaven wide!

5 He shed his blood to pay sin's price,
the full and perfect sacrifice;
as Saviour, reigns eternally,
as Judge of all, presides on high.

6 Lord God, protect us all from sin,
our hearts to love and goodness win;
that we yet firm in faith, shall stay
unshaken in the last great day.

157A
From *Gloria in excelsis*
© Timothy Dudley-Smith

1 All glory be to God on high,
his peace on earth proclaim;
to all his people tell abroad
the grace and glory of the Lord,
and bless his holy name.

2 In songs of thankfulness and praise
our hearts their homage bring
to worship him who reigns above,
almighty Father, Lord of love,
our God and heavenly King.

3 O Christ, the Father's only Son,
O Lamb enthroned on high,
O Jesus, who for sinners died
and reigns at God the Father's side,
in mercy hear our cry.

4 Most high and holy is the Lord,
most high his heavenly throne;
where God the Father, God the Son,
and God the Spirit, ever One,
in glory reigns alone.

157B
Gloria in excelsis, © International
Consultation on English Texts

1 Glory to ' God · in the ' highest:
and ' peace · to his ' people · on ' earth.

2 Lord God ' heaven·ly ' King:
al'mighty ' God and ' Father,

3 we worship you we ' give you ' thanks:
we ' praise you ' for your ' glory.

4 Lord Jesus Christ only ' Son · of the '
Father:
Lord ' God ' Lamb of ' God,

5 you take away the ' sin · of the ' world:
have ' mercy ' on ' us;

6 you are seated at the right hand ' of the '
Father:
re'ceive ' our ' prayer.

7 For you a'lone · are the ' Holy One:
you a'lone ' are the ' Lord,

8 you alone are the Most High *
Jesus Christ with the ' Holy ' Spirit:
**in the glory of God the ' Father. '
A'men.**

157C
From *Gloria in excelsis*
© Christopher Idle/Jubilate Hymns

1 Glory in the highest
to the God of heaven!
Peace to all your people
through the earth be given!
Mighty God and Father,
thanks and praise we bring,
singing Alleluia
to our heavenly king;
singing Alleluia
to our heavenly king.

2 Jesus Christ is risen,
    God the Father's Son!
  With the Holy Spirit
    you are Lord alone!
  Lamb once killed for sinners,
    all our guilt to bear,
  show us now your mercy,
    now receive our prayer;
  show us now your mercy,
    now receive our prayer.

3 Christ the world's true Saviour,
    high and holy One,
  seated now and reigning
    from your Father's throne:
  Lord and God, we praise you!
    Highest heaven adores:
  in the Father's glory,
    all the praise be yours;
  in the Father's glory,
    all the praise be yours!

158A From *Saviour of the world*, © David
Mowbray and Michael Perry/Jubilate Hymns

1 Saviour Christ, in mercy come!
  By your cross and life laid down
  set your waiting people free –
  come among us, Lord, today:

2 Come in power and loose our chains,
  come in peace, forgive our sins,
  come in truth to make us wise,
  come and fill our hearts with praise:

3 Come to live among us, Lord –
  come to save us by your word;
  come today and make us one,
  Saviour Christ, in mercy come!

158B From *Saviour of the world*
© Christopher Idle/Jubilate Hymns

1 Jesus, Saviour of the world,
  you have bought your people's freedom
  by your cross, your life laid down:
  now bring in your glorious kingdom.
    Come to help us!

2 Christ, who once on Galilee
  came to your disciples' rescue:
  we, like them, cry out for help –
  free us from our sins, we ask you.
    Come to save us!

3 Lord, make known
    your promised power;
  show yourself our strong deliverer:
  so our prayer shall turn to praise –
  hear us, stay with us for ever.
    Come to rule us!

4 When you come, Lord Jesus Christ,
  filling earth and heaven with wonder,
  come to make us one with you –
  heirs of life, to reign in splendour.
    Alleluia!

158C *Saviour of the world*
© Joint Liturgical Group

1 Jesus saviour of the world *
  come to us ' in your ' mercy:
  we look to ' you to ' save and ' help us.
2 By your cross and your life laid down *
  you set your ' people ' free:
  we look to ' you to ' save and ' help us.
3 When they were ready to perish you '
  saved · your dis'ciples:
  we look to ' you
  to ' come to · our ' help.
4 In the greatness of your mercy loose us '
  from our ' chains:
  forgive the ' sins of ' all your ' people.
5 Make yourself known as our saviour and '
  mighty · de'liverer:
  save and ' help us ·
  that ' we may ' praise you.
6 Come now and dwell with us ' Lord
  Christ ' Jesus:
  hear our ' prayer ·
  and be ' with us ' always.

Second part
7 And when you ' come in · your ' glory:
  make us to be one with you *
  and to ' share
  the ' life of · your ' kingdom.

158D From *Saviour of the World*
© Joint Liturgical Group

1 LEADER Jesus saviour of the world
            come to us in your mercy:
      MEN we look to you
            to save and help us,
  WOMEN we look to you
            to save and help us.

2 LEADER By your cross
            and your life laid down
            you set your people free:
      MEN we look to you
            to save and help us,
  WOMEN we look to you
            to save and help us.

3   ALL When they were ready to perish
            you saved your disciples:
            we look to you
            to come to our help.

4 In the greatness of your mercy
   loose us from our chains:
   forgive the sins of all your people.

5 LEADER Make yourself known
         as our saviour
         and mighty deliverer:
   MEN   save and help us
         that we may praise you.
   WOMEN save and help us
         that we may praise you.

6 ALL Come now and dwell with us,
        Lord Jesus Christ:
   MEN hear our prayer
        and be with us always,
   WOMEN hear our prayer
        and be with us always.

7 MEN And when you come
        in your glory:
   ALL make us to be one with you
        and to share
        the life of your kingdom,
        your kingdom, your kingdom.

159A
From *Phos hilaron*
© Christopher Idle/Jubilate Hymns

1 Light of gladness, Lord of glory,
   Jesus Christ our king most holy,
   shine among us in your mercy:
      earth and heaven join their hymn.

2 Let us sing at sun's descending
   as we see the lights of evening,
   Father, Son, and Spirit praising
      with the holy seraphim.

3 Son of God, through all the ages
   worthy of our holiest praises,
   yours the life that never ceases,
      light which never shall grow dim.

159B
From *Phos hilaron*
© Paul Inwood/Magnificat Music

1 Light of gladness, shining radiance
   of the heavenly Father's face:
   Jesus Christ, we greet you, bless you,
      holy Lord of saving grace.

2 As the day draws near its ending,
   sunlight dims with fading rays,
   to the Father, Son and Spirit
      now we sing our song of praise.

3 Son of God, the world's redeemer,
   endless praises are your due:
   Lord of life, let all creation
      bring its joyful thanks to you.

159C
From *Phos hilaron*
Robert Bridges (1844–1930)
© in this version Word & Music/
Jubilate Hymns

1 O gladdening light, O grace
   of God the Father's face,
   the eternal splendour wearing:
   celestial, holy, blessed,
   our saviour Jesus Christ,
   (joyful in your appearing,)
   joyful in your appearing.
      (O gladdening light, O grace
      of God the Father's face,
      our saviour Jesus Christ.)

2 As day fades into night
   we see the evening light,
   our hymn of love outpouring;
   Father of might unknown,
   you, his incarnate Son,
   (and Spirit blessed adoring,)
   and Spirit blessed adoring.
      (O gladdening light . . .)

3 To you of right belongs
   the praise of all our songs,
   O Son of God, life-giver;
   you, therefore, Lord most high
   the world shall glorify
   (and shall exalt for ever,)
   and shall exalt for ever.
      (O gladdening light . . .)

160A
From Luke 1, *Song of Mary/Magnificat*
© Christopher Idle/Jubilate Hymns

1 My soul proclaims
         the greatness of the Lord,
   and my spirit sings for joy
         to my saviour God!
   His lowly slave he looked upon in love:
   they will call me happy now,
   for mighty are the works he has done,
   and holy is his name!

2 In every age, for those who fear the Lord
   come his mercy,
         and the strength of his mighty arm;
   he routs the proud,
         throws monarchs off their thrones,
   while he lifts the lowly high,
   fills hungry souls with food,
   and the rich sends empty away.

3 To Israel his servant he brings help,
   and the promise to our fathers
       is now fulfilled:
   for Christ has come
       according to his word,
   and the mercy that he showed
   to Abraham is now
   for his children's children evermore.

160B
From Luke 1, *Song of Mary/Magnificat*
© David Mowbray/Jubilee Hymns

1 With Mary let my soul rejoice,
   and praise God's holy name –
   his saving love from first to last,
   from age to age, the same!

2 How strong his arm, how great his
       power!
   The proud he will disown;
   the meek and humble he exalts
   to share his glorious throne.

3 The rich our God will send away
   and feed the hungry poor;
   the arms of love remain outstretched
   at mercy's open door.

4 So shall God's promise be fulfilled,
   to Israel firmly made:
   a child is born, a Son is given
   whose crown will never fade.

5 All glory to the Father, Son
   and Spirit now proclaim;
   with Mary let the world rejoice
   and praise God's holy name!

160C
From Luke 1, *Song of Mary/Magnificat*
ASB © International Consultation
on English Texts

1 My soul proclaims the ' greatness · of the '
   Lord:
   my spirit re'joices ·
   in ' God my ' saviour;
2 for he has looked with favour on his '
   lowly ' servant:
   from this day
   all gener'ations · will ' call me ' blessed;

Second part
3 the Almighty has done ' great things '
   for me:
   and ' holy ' is his ' name.

4 He has mercy on ' those who ' fear him:
   in ' every ' gener'ation.
5 He has shown the ' strength · of his ' arm:
   he has scattered the ' proud
   in ' their con'ceit.

6 He has cast down the mighty ' from their '
   thrones:
   and has ' lifted ' up the ' lowly.
7 He has filled the hungry with ' good '
   things:
   and the rich he has ' sent a'way '
   empty.
8 He has come to the help of his ' servant '
   Israel:
   for he has re'membered ·
   his ' promise · of ' mercy,
9 the promise he ' made · to our ' fathers:
   to Abraham ' and his ' children ·
   for ' ever.

   Glory to the Father and ' to the ' Son:
   and ' to the ' Holy ' Spirit;
   as it was in the be'ginning · is ' now:
   and shall be for ' ever. ' A'men.

160D
From Luke 1, *Song of Mary/Magnificat*
© Michael Perry/Jubilee Hymns

1 Mary sang a song, a song of love,
   magnified the mighty Lord above;
   melodies of praise his name extol
   from the very depths of Mary's soul:

2 'God the Lord
       has done great things for me,
   looked upon my life's humility;
   happy they shall call me from this day –
   merciful is he whom we obey.

3 'To the humble soul our God is kind,
   to the proud he brings unease of mind.
   Who uplifts the poor,
       pulls down the strong?
   God alone has power to right the wrong!

4 'He who has been Israel's
       strength and stay
   fills the hungry, sends the rich away;
   God has shown his promise
       firm and sure,
   faithful to his people evermore.'

5 This was Mary's song as we recall,
   mother to the saviour of us all:
   magnify his name and sing his praise,
   worship and adore him, all your days!

161A
From *Bless the Lord*
© Christopher Idle/Jubilee Hymns

1 Bless the Lord, our fathers' God,
   bless the name of heaven's king;
   bless him in his holy place,
   tell his praise, his glories sing.

2 Bless the Lord who reigns on high
throned above the cherubim;
bless the Lord who knows the depths,
show his praise and worship him.

3 Bless the Lord for evermore,
bless the Holy Trinity;
bless the Father, Spirit, Son,
sing his praise eternally!

161B/C
Bless the Lord
© Joint Liturgical Group

1 Bless the Lord the ' God of · our ' fathers:
**sing his ' praise ·
and ex'alt him · for ' ever.**

2 Bless his holy and ' glori·ous ' name:
**sing his ' praise ·
and ex'alt him · for ' ever.**

3 Bless him in his holy and ' glori·ous '
temple:
**sing his ' praise ·
and ex'alt him · for ' ever.**

4 Bless him who be'holds the ' depths:
**sing his ' praise ·
and ex'alt him · for ' ever.**

5 Bless him who sits be'tween the '
cherubim:
**sing his ' praise ·
and ex'alt him · for ' ever.**

6 Bless him on the ' throne of · his '
kingdom:
**sing his ' praise ·
and ex'alt him · for ' ever.**

7 Bless him in the ' heights of ' heaven:
**sing his ' praise ·
and ex'alt him · for ' ever.**

8 Bless the Father the Son
and the ' Holy ' Spirit:
**sing his ' praise ·
and ex'alt him · for ' ever.**

162A
From Luke 2, *Song of Simeon/*
Nunc dimittis © Timothy Dudley-Smith

1 Faithful vigil ended,
watching, waiting cease:
Master, grant your servant
his discharge in peace.

2 All the Spirit promised,
all the Father willed,
now these eyes behold it
perfectly fulfilled.

3 This your great deliverance
sets your people free;
Christ their light uplifted
all the nations see.

4 Christ, your people's glory!
watching, doubting cease:
grant to us your servants
our discharge in peace.

162B
From Luke 2, *Song of Simeon/*
Nunc dimittis, J E Seddon
© Mrs M Seddon/Jubilate Hymns

1 Lord, now let your servant
go his way in peace –
your great love has brought me
joy that will not cease:

2 For my eyes have seen him
promised from of old –
saviour of all people,
shepherd of one fold:

3 Light of revelation
to the gentiles shown,
light of Israel's glory
to the world made known.

162C
From Luke 2, *Song of Simeon/*
Nunc dimittis © International Consultation
on English Texts

1 Lord now you let your servant ' go in '
peace:
your ' word has ' been ful'filled.

2 My own eyes have ' seen the · sal'vation:
**which you have prepared
in the ' sight of ' every ' people;**

3 a light to re'veal you · to the ' nations:
**and the ' glory ·
of your ' people ' Israel.**

**Glory to the Father and ' to the ' Son:
and ' to the ' Holy ' Spirit;
as it was in the be'ginning · is ' now:
and shall be for ' ever. ' A'men.**

162D
From Luke 2,
Song of Simeon/Nunc dimittis
© Michael Saward/Jubilate Hymns

1 Now at last
your servant can depart in peace,
for your word
is finally fulfilled:

2 My own eyes
have witnessed your salvation, Lord,
which is seen
throughout the waiting world,

3 Light for all,
   revealing you to every land;
   glorious sight,
   your people Israel's hope.

4 Praises be
   to God the Father, Spirit, Son –
   Three-in-One,
   the God whom we adore!

162E From Luke 2,
Song of Simeon/Nunc dimittis
© Michael Perry/Jubilate Hymns

1 Jesus, hope of every nation,
   light of heaven upon our way;
   promise of the world's salvation,
   spring of life's eternal day!

2 Saints by faith on God depending
   wait to see Messiah born;
   sin's oppressive night is ending
   in the glory of the dawn!

3 Look, he comes! – the long-awaited
   Christ, redeemer, living Word;
   hope and faith are vindicated
   as with joy we greet the Lord.

4 Glory in the highest heaven
   to the Father, Spirit, Son;
   and on earth let praise be given
   to our God, the Three-in-One!

163A From Philippians 2, *Song of Christ's Glory*
F B Tucker, © The Church Pension Fund

1 All praise to Christ,
      our Lord and king divine,
   yielding your glory in your love's design,
   that in our darkened hearts your grace
         might shine:
      Alleluia!

2 You came to us in lowliness of thought;
   by you the outcast and the poor
         were sought,
   and by your death
         was our redemption bought:
      Alleluia!

3 The mind of Christ
      is as our mind should be –
   he was a servant, that we might be free;
   humbling himself to death on Calvary:
      Alleluia!

4 And so we see in God's great purpose,
         how
   Christ has been raised
         above all creatures now;
   and at his name shall every nation bow:
      Alleluia!

5 Let every tongue confess
      with one accord,
   in heaven and earth,
      that Jesus Christ is Lord,
   and God the Father be by all adored:
      Alleluia! (Amen.)

163B From Philippians 2, *Song of Christ's Glory*
© Brian Black and Word & Music/
Jubilate Hymns

1 Before the heaven and earth
   were made by God's decree,
   the Son of God all-glorious dwelt
   in God's eternity.

2 Though in the form of God
   and rich beyond compare,
   he did not think to grasp his prize;
   nor did he linger there.

3 From heights of heaven he came
   to this world full of sin,
   to meet with hunger, hatred, hell –
   our life, our love to win.

4 The Son became true Man
   and took a servant's role;
   with lowliness and selfless love
   he came, to make us whole.

5 Obedient to his death –
   that death upon a cross,
   no son had ever shown such love,
   nor father known such loss.

6 To him enthroned on high,
   by angel hosts adored,
   all knees shall bow, and tongues confess
   that Jesus Christ is Lord.

163C From Philippians 2, *Song of Christ's Glory*
© Church of the Province of South Africa

1 Christ Jesus was in the ' form of ' God:
   **but he did not ' cling ·
      to e'quality · with ' God.**
2 He emptied himself * taking the ' form. ·
   of a ' servant:
   **and was ' born ·
      in the ' likeness · of ' men.**
3 Being found in human form he ' humbled ·
   him'self:
   **and became obedient unto death '
      even · death · on a ' cross.**
4 Therefore God has ' highly · ex'alted him:
   **and bestowed on him
      the ' name a·bove ' every ' name,**

5 that at the name of Jesus every ˈ knee
should ˈ bow:
**in heaven and on ˈ earth
and ˈ under · the ˈ earth;**
6 and every tongue confess that Jesus ˈ
Christ is ˈ Lord:
to the ˈ glory · of ˈ God the ˈ Father.

**Glory to the Father and ˈ to the ˈ Son:
and ˈ to the ˈ Holy ˈ Spirit;
as it was in the beˈginning · is ˈ now:
and shall be for ˈ ever. ˈ Aˈmen.**

163D
From Philippians 2, *Song of Christ's Glory*
© Stephen Horsfall/Jubilate Hymns

1 Though Christ put on our frail humanity,
he was in very truth our God and king;
and yet he did not claim equality,
but trod the path of humble suffering.

2 As God and man
he chose the way to death,
bearing our sins upon the cruel cross;
he blessed his killers
with his dying breath,
his agony redeemed our grievous loss.

3 Since for our sake he gladly went to die,
taking upon himself our race's shame,
God raised him, and exalted him on high,
gave him the highest place
and holiest name:

4 So at the name of Jesus, every knee
in heaven, on earth and in the depths,
should bow;
and every tongue confess that only he
is Lord.
Come, let us praise his glory now!

163E
From Philippians 2, *Song of Christ's Glory*
© Michael Perry/Jubilate Hymns

1 Down from the height of his glory
he came,
willingly leaving his rightful domain:
Jesus was born in the image of man;
love was his motive and mercy his aim.

2 All through those days
his resolve was the same –
Jesus the servant, the sharer of pain:
perfect obedience, the path of disdain,
down to a death of derision and shame.

3 Now God has granted him
honour and fame,
taken him up to the highest to reign:
'Jesus is Lord!' every voice shall maintain,
all of creation shall bow to his name.

164A
From Revelation 4, 5 *Glory and honour*
© Timothy Dudley-Smith

1 Heavenly hosts in ceaseless worship
'Holy, holy, holy!' cry;
'He who is, who was and will be,
God almighty, Lord most high.'
Praise and honour, power and glory,
be to him who reigns alone!
We, with all his hands have fashioned,
fall before the Father's throne.

2 All creation, all redemption,
join to sing the saviour's worth;
Lamb of God whose blood has bought us,
kings and priests, to reign on earth.
Wealth and wisdom, power and glory,
honour, might, dominion, praise,
now be his from all his creatures
and to everlasting days!

164B
From Revelation 4, 5 *Glory and honour*
© Michael Perry/Jubilate Hymns

1 Glory and honour,
wisdom and splendour,
Lord of creation,
are yours alone:
all of earth's creatures
in exultation
sing to the Lamb upon the throne.

2 Once was the ransom
paid for our freedom –
from every nation
with you we reign:
yours be the praises,
high veneration,
worship for evermore. Amen.

164C
From Revelation 4, 5 *Glory and honour*
© Joint Liturgical Group

1 Glory and ˈ honour · and ˈ power:
are yours by ˈ right O ˈ Lord our ˈ God:

2 for you creˈated ˈ all things:
**and by your ˈ will
they ˈ have their ˈ being.**

3 Glory and ˈ honour · and ˈ power:
**are yours by ˈ right
O ˈ Lamb · who was ˈ slain;**

4 for by your blood you ransomed ˈ us for ˈ
God:
from every race and language *
from ˈ every ˈ people · and ˈ nation,

5 to make us a ˈ kingdom · of ˈ priests:
to stand and ˈ serve beˈfore our ˈ God.

To him who sits on the throne ' and ·
to the ' Lamb:
be praise and honour
glory and might *
for ever and ' ever. ' A'men.

164D   From Revelation 4, 5, *Glory and honour*
                      © Joint Liturgical Group

ALL
Glory and honour and power
are yours by right,
O Lord our God;
glory and honour and power
are yours by right,
O Lamb that was slain:

For you created all things,
and by your will they have their being.
    Glory and honour . . .

For by your blood
        you ransomed us for God
from every race and language,
from every people and nation:
    Glory and honour . . .

To make us a kingdom of priests;
to stand and serve before our God.
    Glory and honour . . .

To him who sits on the throne
        and to the Lamb,
be praise and honour, glory and might
        for ever and ever!
    Glory and honour . . .

164E   From Revelation 4, 5, *Glory and honour*
                      © Christopher Idle/Jubilate Hymns

Come and see the shining hope
        that Christ's apostle saw;
on the earth, confusion
        but in heaven an open door,
where the living creatures
        praise the Lamb for evermore:
Love has the victory for ever!
    Amen, he comes!
    to bring his own reward!
    Amen, praise God!
    for justice now restored;
    kingdoms of the world become
    the kingdom of the Lord:
Love has the victory for ever!

2   All the gifts you send us, Lord,
        are faithful, good and true;
    holiness and righteousness
        are shown in all you do:
    who can see your greatest Gift
        and fail to worship you?
    Love has the victory for ever!
        Amen, he comes . . .

3   Power and salvation
        all belong to God on high!
    So the mighty multitudes of heaven
        make their cry,
    singing Alleluia!
        where the echoes never die:
    Love has the victory for ever!
        Amen, he comes . . .

164F   From Revelation 4, 5, *Glory and honour*
                      © Michael Perry/Jubilate Hymns

1   Glory, glory, glory to the Lord;
    glory to the Lord God almighty:
    for you created all that is.
    Glory, glory, glory to the Lord!

2   Honour, honour, honour to the Lamb;
    honour to the Lord God almighty:
    for by your blood you ransomed us.
    Honour, honour, honour to the Lamb!

3   Power, power, power to the Lord;
    power to the Lord God almighty:
    for you have made us kings and priests.
    Power, power, power to the Lord!

165A   From *Te Lucis ante terminum*
                      © in this version Jubilate Hymns

1   Before the ending of the day,
    Creator of the world, we pray:
    protect us by your mighty grace,
    grant us your mercy and your peace:

2   Bless us in sleep, that we may find
    no terrors to disturb our mind;
    our cunning enemy restrain –
    guard us from sin and all its stain.

3   O Father, may your will be done
    through Jesus Christ your only Son;
    whom with the Spirit we adore,
    one God, both now and evermore.

165B   From *Te Lucis ante terminum*
                      © Michael Perry/Jubilate Hymns

1   Now evening comes to close the day,
    and soon the silent hours
    shall banish all our fears away,
    and sleep renew our powers.

2 Into your hands, eternal Friend,
  we give ourselves again,
  and to your watchful care commend
  all those in grief or pain.

3 In waking, lift our thoughts above,
  in sleeping, guard us still,
  that we may rise to know your love
  and prove your perfect will.

4 To Father, Son and Spirit – praise,
  all mortal praise be given,
  till sleep at last shall end our days
  and we shall wake in heaven!

166
From *Exsultet* (Easter song of praise)
© Christopher Idle/Jubilate Hymns

1 Exult, creation round God's throne!
  All heaven, rejoice! All angels, sing!
  Salvation's trumpet sound aloud
  for Jesus Christ, our risen king.

2 Exult, O earth, in radiant hope;
  in Christ's majestic splendour shine!
  The Lord is here, the victory won,
  the darkness drowned in light divine.

3 Exult, all Christians, one in praise
  with our Jerusalem above!
  This roof shall ring with Easter songs
  that echo Christ's redeeming love.

OPTIONAL VERSE
  Exult in God, pure well of truth;
  in Christ, fresh fountainhead of grace;
  in Spirit, flowing stream of life –
  eternal Joy our hearts embrace.

167
From Exodus 15, *The Easter Liturgy*
© Christopher Idle/Jubilate Hymns

1 I will sing the Lord's high triumph,
  ruling earth and sky and sea;
  God, my strength, my song, my glory,
  my salvation now is he.
    Through the waters,
    through the waters,
  (God has brought us liberty,)
  God has brought us liberty.

2 By the storm and at the mountain
  grace and judgement both are shown;
  all who planned his people's ruin
  power divine has overthrown.
    Nations tremble,
    nations tremble;
  (God has made his mercy known,)
  God has made his mercy known.

3 Who is like the God of Israel,
  faithful, holy, throned above?
  Stretching out the arm of anger,
  yet he guides us by his love.
    To our homeland,
    to our homeland,
  (God will see us safely move,)
  God will see us safely move.

4 Praise our God, who in his thunder
  led a nation through the sea;
  praise the one whose blood released us
  from our deeper slavery.
    Alleluia,
    alleluia,
  (Christ is risen: we are free;)
  Christ is risen: we are free!

168
From *Gloria*

Glory to the Father, and to the Son,
and to the Holy Spirit:
as it was in the beginning, is now,
and shall be for ever. Amen.

Legal Information, Notes and Acknowledgements

salm versions and Liturgical Texts

hose seeking to reprint material in this book which is the property of .bilate Hymns or associated authors (attributed '/Jubilate Hymns') may write
   The Copyright Secretary, Jubilate Hymns Ltd, 61 Chessel Avenue, uthampton SO2 4DY. In the United States of America these copyrights and .ose of Timothy Dudley-Smith, Fred Kaan and Fred Pratt Green are lministered by Hope Publishing Company, Carol Stream, Illinois 60188. ddresses of other copyright-holders can also be supplied.

Jubilate Hymns, Marshall Pickering Communications, Scripture Union, hankyou Music, Word (UK) Ltd – along with other copyright-holders whose les they administer (Celebration Services, Maranatha!, Word & Music etc.) ave uniform concessions and rates. Details are available from the Copyright ecretary, Jubilate Hymns Ltd.

Most of these publishers also combine to offer a licensing scheme for nited term reproduction. Where this is felt to be an advantage, application 1ould be made to the Christian Music Association at Glyndley Manor, Stone ross, Pevensey, East Sussex BN24 5BS (0320 440440). Hymns copyrighted ainer & Bell may not be reprinted or photocopied under any blanket :ensing scheme, but should be cleared individually with Stainer & Bell .mited. Full details and addresses of copyright-holders may be found under .ch item in the music editions of *Psalms for Today* and *Songs from the* .alms.

iturgical (Responsive) Psalms

hese texts are the copyright of the Editor, and are available for local production subject to acknowledgement of source in the form 'Reprinted om *Psalms for Today* with the permission of Jubilate Hymns Ltd' (or, in the .A, ' . . . of Hope Publishing Company, Carol Stream, Illinois 60188').

ecording and Broadcasting

.bilate Hymns and associated authors, and Word & Music are members of .e Mechanical Copyright Protection and Performing Right Societies.

he Alternative Service Book

he Alternative Service Book 1980 (ASB) is © the Central Board of Finance of .e Church of England 1980.

The content of Holy Communion Rite A and Morning or Evening Worship is rawn from alternative services authorised for use in the Church of England. he complete alternative services of Holy Communion Rite A, Morning rayer and Evening Prayer may be found in ASB. These services are

Acknowledgements

We owe our thanks most particularly to those authors and composers who readily created or adapted their work to meet the need for fluent and congregational texts and music settings of quality and relative simplicity. We mention especially those to whom we turned time and again for help and support: John Barnard, Timothy Dudley-Smith, Brian Foley, Christopher Idle, David Mowbray, Christopher Norton, Chris Rolinson, Norman Warren and Paul Wigmore.

For application of her special expertise to the text of liturgical (responsive) psalms we thank Rev. Dr. Kathleen Bowe of Cliff College.

For the major task of copyright clearance and assistance in preparing the work for publication we thank Bunty Grundy of Jubilate Hymns. For their encouragement and professionalism we acknowledge the contribution of publishers and typesetters – especially Hodder and Stoughton's Tim Anderson, Dick Douglas and Kathy Dyke, and Barnes' Michael Mack Smith.

Michael Perry (Editor)

Index of First Lines

Spoken ('Liturgical') Psalms are not listed here

The Order for Holy Communion Rite A

from the Alternative Service Book 1980

The Prayers of the Congregation

THE PREPARATION

The Lord be with you
and also with you.

**Almighty God,
to whom all hearts are open,
all desires known,
and from whom no secrets are hidden:
cleanse the thoughts of our hearts
by the inspiration of your Holy Spirit,
that we may perfectly love you,
and worthily magnify your holy name;
through Christ our Lord.   Amen.**

There is no other commandment greater
than these.
Amen. Lord have mercy.

**Almighty God, our heavenly Father,
we have sinned against you
    and against our fellow men,
in thought and word and deed,
through negligence, through weakness,
through our own deliberate fault.
We are truly sorry,
and repent of all our sins.
For the sake of your Son Jesus Christ
    who died for us,
forgive us all that is past;
and grant that we may serve you
    in newness of life
to the glory of your name.   Amen.**

Or

**Almighty God, our heavenly Father,
we have sinned against you,
through our own fault,
in thought and word and deed,
and in what we have left undone.
For your Son our Lord Jesus Christ's
    sake,
forgive us all that is past;
and grant that we may serve you
    in newness of life
to the glory of your name.   Amen.**

Lord, have mercy.   Christ, have mercy.
Lord, have mercy.   **Christ, have mercy.**

Lord, have mercy.
Lord, have mercy.

**Glory to God in the highest,
and peace to his people on earth.**

**Lord God, heavenly King,
almighty God and Father,
we worship you, we give you thanks,
we praise you for your glory.**

**Lord Jesus Christ,
    only Son of the Father,
Lord God, Lamb of God,
you take away the sin of the world:
have mercy on us:
you are seated at the right hand
    of the Father:
receive our prayer.**

**For you alone are the Holy One,
you alone are the Lord,
you alone are the Most High,
Jesus Christ,
with the Holy Spirit,
in the glory of God the Father.   Amen.**

THE MINISTRY OF THE WORD

This is the word of the Lord.
Thanks be to God.

Glory to Christ our Saviour.

This is the Gospel of Christ.
Praise to Christ our Lord.

**We believe in one God,
the Father, the almighty,
maker of heaven and earth,
of all that is,
seen and unseen.**

**We believe in one Lord, Jesus Christ,
the only Son of God,
eternally begotten of the Father,
God from God, Light from Light,
true God from true God,
begotten, not made,
of one Being with the Father.
Through him all things were made.
For us and for our salvation
he came down from heaven;
by the power of the Holy Spirit
he became incarnate of the Virgin Mary,
    and was made man.**

For our sake he was crucified
    under Pontius Pilate;
he suffered death and was buried.
On the third day he rose again
in accordance with the Scriptures;
he ascended into heaven
and is seated at the right hand
    of the Father
He will come again in glory
to judge the living and the dead,
and his kingdom will have no end.

We believe in the Holy Spirit,
the Lord, the giver of life,
who proceeds from the Father
    and the Son.
With the Father and the Son
    he is worshipped and glorified.
He has spoken through the Prophets.

We believe in one holy catholic
    and apostolic Church.
We acknowledge one baptism
    for the forgiveness of sins.
We look for the resurrection of the dead,
and the life of the world to come.   Amen.

Lord in your mercy
hear our prayer.

Merciful Father,
accept these prayers
for the sake of your Son,
our Saviour Jesus Christ.   Amen.

We do not presume
to come to this your table, merciful Lord,
trusting in our own righteousness,
but in your manifold and great mercies.
We are not worthy
so much as to gather up the crumbs
    under your table.
But you are the same Lord
whose nature is always to have mercy.
Grant us therefore, gracious Lord,
so to eat the flesh of your dear Son
    Jesus Christ
and to drink his blood,
that we may evermore dwell in him
and he in us.   Amen.

Or

Most merciful Lord,
your love compels us to come in.
Our hands were unclean,
our hearts were unprepared;

we were not fit
even to eat the crumbs
    from under your table.
But you, Lord
    are the God of our salvation,
and share your bread with sinners.
So cleanse and feed us
with the precious body and blood
    of your Son,
that he may live in us and we in him;
and that we,
    with the whole company of Christ,
may sit and eat in your kingdom.   Amen.

THE MINISTRY OF THE SACRAMENT

The peace of the Lord be always with you
and also with you.

Yours, Lord, is the greatness, the power,
the glory, the splendour, and the majesty;
for everything in heaven and on earth
    is yours.
All things come from you,
and of your own do we give you.

The Lord is here.
His Spirit is with us.

Lift up your hearts.
We lift them to the Lord.

Let us give thanks to the Lord our God.
It is right to give him thanks and praise.

We proclaim your great and glorious name,
for ever praising you and saying:
Holy, holy, holy Lord,
God of power and might,
heaven and earth are full of your glory.
Hosanna in the highest.

Blessed is he who comes
    in the name of the Lord.
Hosanna in the highest.

Do this, as often as you drink it,
in remembrance of me.
Christ has died:
Christ is risen:
Christ will come again.

(We worship you, Father almighty,
in songs of everlasting praise:
Blessing and honour and glory and power
be yours for ever and ever.)

Amen.

As our Saviour taught us, so we pray.
Our Father in heaven,
hallowed be your name,
your kingdom come,
your will be done,
on earth as in heaven.
Give us today our daily bread.
Forgive us our sins
as we forgive those who sin against us.
Lead us not into temptation
but deliver us from evil.

For the kingdom, the power,
and the glory are yours
now and for ever.   Amen.

We break this bread
to share in the body of Christ.
Though we are many, we are one body,
because we all share in one bread.

AFTER COMMUNION

Father of all,
we give you thanks and praise,
that when we were still far off
you met us in your Son
   and brought us home.
Dying and living,
he declared your love,
gave us grace,
and opened the gate of glory.

May we who share Christ's body
live his risen life;
we who drink his cup
bring life to others;
we whom the Spirit lights
give light to the world.
Keep us firm
in the hope you have set before us
so we and all your children
   shall be free,
and the whole earth
live to praise your name;
through Christ our Lord.   **Amen.**

Almighty God,
we thank you for feeding us
with the body and blood of your Son
   Jesus Christ
Through him we offer you
   our souls and bodies
to be a living sacrifice.
Send us out
in the power of your Spirit
to live and work
to your praise and glory.   Amen.

Go in peace to love and serve the Lord.
In the name of Christ.   Amen.

Or

Go in the peace of Christ.
Thanks be to God.

Morning or Evening Worship

drawn from the Alternative
Service Book 1980

INTRODUCTION

We have come together
as the family of God
in our Father's presence
to offer him praise and thanksgiving,
to hear and receive his holy word,
to bring before him
the needs of the world,
to ask forgiveness of our sins,
and to seek his grace,
that through his Son Jesus Christ
we may give ourselves to his service.

SENTENCE

If we say we have no sin,
we deceive ourselves,
and the truth is not in us.
If we confess our sins,
God is faithful and just,
and will forgive us our sins,
and cleanse us
from all unrighteousness.

CONFESSION

Let us confess our sins to almighty God:
**Almighty God, our heavenly Father,
we have sinned against you
and against our fellow men,
in thought and word and deed,
through negligence,
through weakness,
through our own deliberate fault.
We are truly sorry
and repent of all our sins.
For the sake of your Son Jesus Christ,
who died for us,
forgive us all that is past;
and grant that we may serve you
in newness of life
to the glory of your name. Amen.**

Or

**Almighty God, our heavenly Father,
we have sinned against you,
through our own fault,
in thought and word and deed,
and in what we have left undone.**

**For your Son our Lord Jesus Christ's sake,
forgive us all that is past;
and grant that we may serve you
in newness of life
to the glory of your name. Amen.**

ABSOLUTION

Almighty God, who forgives all who truly
repent, have mercy upon *you*, pardon and
deliver *you* from all *your* sins, confirm and
strengthen *you* in all goodness, and keep
you in life eternal; through Jesus Christ our
Lord. **Amen.**

LITANY

O Lord, open our lips:
**and our mouth shall proclaim
your praise.**

Let us worship the Lord:
all praise to his name.

**Glory to the Father, and to the Son,
and to the Holy Spirit:
as it was in the beginning, is now,
and shall be for ever. Amen.**

RESPONSE TO READINGS

This is the word of the Lord:
thanks be to God.

THE APOSTLES' CREED

**I believe in God, the Father almighty,
creator of heaven and earth.
I believe in Jesus Christ, his only Son,
our Lord.
He was conceived by the power
of the Holy Spirit
and born of the Virgin Mary.
He suffered under Pontius Pilate,
was crucified, died and was buried.
He descended to the dead.
On the third day he rose again.
He ascended into heaven,
and is seated at the right hand
of the Father.
He will come again
to judge the living and the dead.
I believe in the Holy Spirit,
the holy catholic Church,
the communion of saints,
the forgiveness of sins,
the resurrection of the body,
and the life everlasting. Amen.**

Lord have mercy upon us.
Christ have mercy upon us.
Lord have mercy upon us.

THE LORD'S PRAYER
**Our Father in heaven,
hallowed be your name,
your kingdom come,
your will be done,
on earth as in heaven.
Give us today our daily bread.
Forgive us our sins
as we forgive those
     who sin against us.
Lead us not into temptation
but deliver us from evil.**

**For the kingdom, the power,
     and the glory are yours
now and for ever.   Amen.**

RESPONSES
Show us your mercy, O Lord;
and grant us your salvation.

O Lord save the Queen;
and teach her counsellors wisdom.

Let your priests be clothed with
righteousness;
and let your servants shout for joy.

O Lord, make your ways known upon the
earth;
**let all nations acknowledge
     your saving power.**

Give your people the blessing of peace;
and let your glory be over all the world.

Make our hearts clean, O God;
and renew a right spirit within us.

MORNING COLLECTS
Almighty and everlasting Father,
we thank you
that you have brought us safely
to the beginning of this day.
Keep us from falling into sin
or running into danger;
order us in all our doings;
and guide us to do always
what is right in your eyes;
through Jesus Christ our Lord.   **Amen.**

Or

Eternal God and Father,
you create us by your power
and redeem us by your love:
guide and strengthen us by your Spirit,
that we may give ourselves
     in love and service
to one another and to you;
through Jesus Christ our Lord.   **Amen.**

EVENING COLLECT
Lighten our darkness,
Lord, we pray;
and in your mercy defend us
from all perils and dangers of this night;
for the love of your only Son
our Saviour Jesus Christ.   **Amen.**